The Royal Emblem
(reproduced on the cover)

The Royal Emblem is divided into five fields with a purple coat-of-arms in the middle showing a silver, two-tailed crowned lion (Bohemia). The first field is blue bearing a crowned, silver-and-purple-chequered eagle (Moravia). In the second, upon a golden background, there is a black-crowned eagle bearing on her bosom a crescent ended with a trefoil and a cross (Silesia). In the third, there is a golden wall (Upper Lužice), in the fourth, on a blue background, there is a golden eagle (Těšín area) and in the fifth, on a silver background, there is a purple bull shown in later paintings as standing on a green lawn (Lower Lužice) respectively. Round the coat-of-arms, there is a purple throne with the St. Václav's crown set upon it.

Karlštejn

Medieval arrangement following to adaptation made in the first half of the 16th century.

© INFOA
ISBN 80 - 85836 - 27 - 0

CZECH HISTORY
Chronological Survey

AUTHORS

Jaroslav Krejčíř, Ing. Stanislav Soják

EDITORS OF THE CHRONOLOGICAL PART

PhDr. František Spurný Csc., PhDr. Dan Gawrecki Csc.
Mgr. Ivana Fuxová, PhDr. Zdeněk Jirásek Csc.

TRANSLATOR

Dr. Jan Mynařík

ILLUSTRATORS

Pavel Alexander Taťoun
Zdeněk Skřivánek
Lenka Suchá
Petr Herzig

INFOA

Praotec Čech

CZECH HISTORY

Chronological Survey

Sovereigns and heads of the state (nation)	Territorial, national and judiciary background	Other remarkable events
approximately since the fourth century before Christ	Czech territories settled (inhabited) by Celts approx. since the fourth century before Christ (Bois in Bohemia, Cotins in Moravia).	
by the beginning of our era	German tribes (Marcomans in Bohemia, Quads in Moravia). Rise of a great realm extending from Danube to Visla. 180 - 374 Quads subjected to Romans.	166 - 180 Marcoman wars led by Marcus Aurelius.
434 - 453 ATTILA	Both Marcomans and Quads subjected to Huns. Up to 500 intermittent settlements of German Langobards, Goths, Vandals, Heruls and Skirs. By 500, most Marcomans left from Bohemia to Bavaria, and, since the second century after Christ, supposed arrival of Slavs (apparently earlier in Moravia than in Bohemia). The latter set up tribal principalities of Czechs, Croatians, Lucans, Zlicans etc.	451 Huns defeated by Romans, Burgunds, Visigots and Francs in the Catalaunian fields.

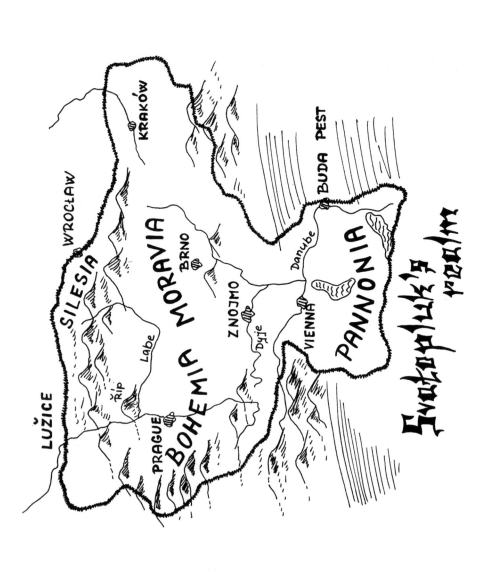

558 - 603 BAJAN	Avars' hegemony (Turkish- Tatarian tribes of Asia).	
623 - 658 SAMO (Legends on Krok, Libuše, Přemysl and seven Premyslides.)	Rise of a great Slav "realm" governed by Samo, the Franc merchant, whose extent was most likely associated with both the Bohemian and Moravian territories, the real extent being more or less hypothetical.	
830 - 846 MOJMÍR I reigning over Great Moravia	Mojmír I founded the realm called Great Moravia with south-Moravian valleys as its core. He attached Great Mora- via to the Nitra region, up to then governed by Pribina.	In 800 Charles the Great's coronation as the Pope of Rome. In 805 Charles the Great's expedition to Bohemia. In 845 fourteen Czech knights baptized in the court of the East -Franc king Ludvig the German in Regensburg.
846 - 870 ROSTISLAV Mojmír's nephew, reigning over Great Moravia	After Mojmír's death, his nephew Rostislav ascended to the thro- ne. He tried to shake off the influence of the East-Franc realm and switched over to the Bysan- thinian. He called Constantin and Method, Bysanthinian missionaries to Moravia. The East-Franc king Ludvig the German undertook military expeditions to Moravia, the latter, however, kept its inde- pendence.	863 Constantin and Method in Moravia. Method (became) Archbishop of Moravia and Panonia. 869/870 restoration of St. Andronic's archdiocese with Method as archbishop.
870 - 894 SVATOPLUK Rostislav's nephew, reigning over Great Moravia	Franc forces undertook many invasions in both Bohemia and Moravia. With Svatopluk leading them, Moravians resisted suc- cessfully Francs and undertook expansive expeditions into surrounding countries. In those days, Great Moravia acquired	885 Slav liturgy introduced for simple folks in order to clarify Gospel and Epistles.

Knight Václav

largest territory extending from Lužice to Hungary.

? - 889 / 890
BOŘIVOJ I,
the Premyslide,
Knight of Bohemia

Bořivoj acknowledged Svatopluk's supremacy. After his death, Bohemia stood under direct reign of Svatopluk. 890 East-Franc King Arnulf approved Svatopluk's supremacy over Czech tribes.

886 victory of Latin liturgy adherents.

894 - 906
MOJMÍR II,
Svatopluk's son,
sovereign over
Great Moravia

895 Bohemia's separation from Great Moravia. Heralds of Czech tribes with Spytihněv, the Premyslide at their head, taking fidelity oaths to Arnulf, the East-Franc sovereign.

SVATOPLUK II,
brother of Mojmír II,
charged with administration
of the Nitra area

905 East Moravia (Slovakia) occupied by Hungarians. Prior to 907, Great Moravia destroyed by Hungarian invasions.

? - 915
SPYTIHNĚV,
Bořivoj's son,
Knight of Bohemia

Foundation of churches in Prague castle and Budeč areas ascribed to Spytihněv.

915 - 921
VRATISLAV,
Spytihněv's brother,
Knight of Bohemia

Vratislav's successful protection of Bohemia against Hungarian impacts. Marrying Drahomíra (from Stodoran tribe), he strove for union with other West-Slav tribes.

921 - 924
DRAHOMÍRA,
Vratislav's spouse

Drahomíra assumed tutor's reign for the sake of minor Vratislav's son Václav, predetermined as a Czech knight during his father's lifetime.

921 Ludmila, knight Bořivoj's widow, murdered on order of Drahomíra. Ludmila was later sanctified.

9

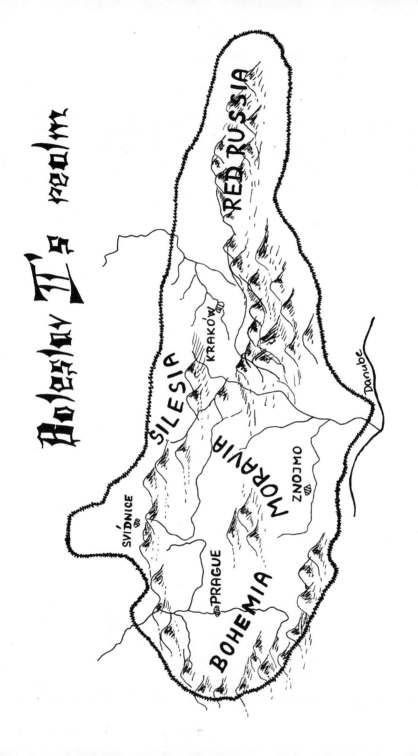

Boleslav II's realm

924 - 935 VÁCLAV, Vratislav's son, knight of Bohemia	Henry I, German king, together with Arnulf, King of Bavaria, undertook invasion to Bohemia. Knight Václav's subjection to the German sovereign.	935 Knight Václav assassinated in Stará Boleslav on his brother Boleslav's order. Václav was later sanctified and patronized.
935 - 972 BOLESLAV I, Václav's brother, knight of Bohemia	Fourteen years' struggle with German realm. Though unbeaten, Boleslav forced by enemy to negotiations. Boleslav surrendered acknowledging supremacy of Otto I, German king and later Roman emperor. Both Boleslav I and Boleslav II's expeditions expanded the power of Premyslide house to Silesia, Cracow and Mainz areas, most likely Moravia, Red Russia and western Slovakia respectively.	955 Hungarian's defeat on Lech River. 962 Otto I coronated Roman emperor. Rise of Medieval Roman Empire; until the 16th century of Saint Roman Empire of the German Nation. 965 Boleslav I's daughter Doubravka married to Mieshek Piastow, Polish sovereign.
972 - 999 BOLESLAV II, son of Boleslav I, knight of Bohemia	995 conquest of Libice (upon Cidlina) castle area and massacring all of the Slavniko-vites present. This deed accomplished Bohemia's unification under Premyslides' rule.	973 Prague diocese foundation. Rise of first monasteries. 997 Assassination of Vojtěch, Bishop of Prague, one of the most learned men of that period. Later sanctified.
999 - 1002 BOLESLAV III, son of Boleslav II, knight of Bohemia	Boleslav III lost Cracow area, Silesia and Moravia, gained after victorious military expeditions by Boleslav the Valiant, Polish sovereign. 1002 Boleslav III dethroned and expatriated. 1003 the latter reassumed his power. Jaroslav and Oldřich, his brothers, left Bohemia settling down in the Court of Heinrich III, Duke of Bavaria.	

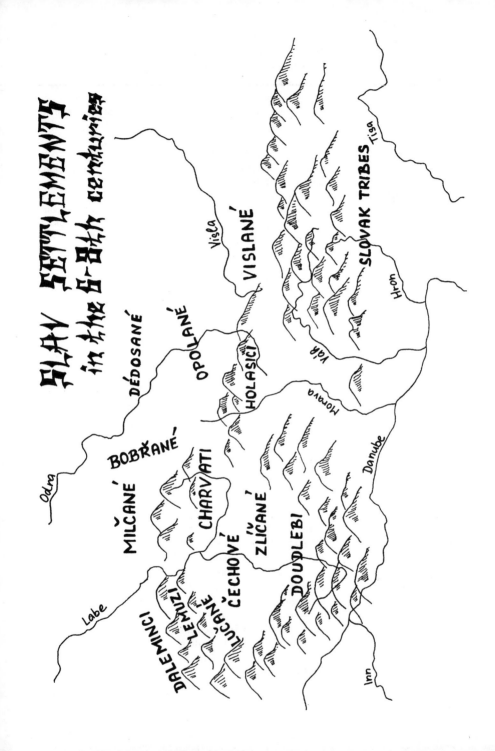

1002 - 1003
VLADIVOJ,
Knight of Bohemia

Vladivoj, affiliated with Premyslide House, not markedly interfered with Czech history.

1003
JAROMÍR,
brother of Boleslav III,
Knight of Bohemia

Boleslav III's brothers Jaromír and Oldřich, returned to Bohemia after leaving Bavaria, the former assuming the reign for a short period of time. Boleslav the Valiant, Polish sovereign, assisted Boleslav III in reassuming reign in Bohemia. Both Jaromír and Oldřich compelled to leave the country again.

1003
BOLESLAV III,
son of Boleslav II,
Knight of Bohemia

Fearing conspiracy Boleslav III massacred barons from the House of Vršovec. Boleslav the Valiant, Knight of Poland, captured Czech sovereign and deprived him of sight.

1003 - 1004
BOLESLAV
THE VALIANT,
brother of Vladivoj,
Knight of Poland
and Bohemia

After imprisoning Boleslav III, Boleslav the Valiant usurped reign in Bohemia. Prior to that, he dominated Moravia as well. Rise of Polish - Czech realm.

1004 - 1012
JAROMÍR,
brother of Boleslav III,
Knight of Bohemia

Heinrich II, King of Germany, undertook military invasion of Bohemia. Due to Jaromír, who participated therein, he succeeded in chasing the Polish out of Bohemia; Moravia remained under Polish supremacy. 1004 Jaromír proclaimed (for the second time) knight of Bohemia.

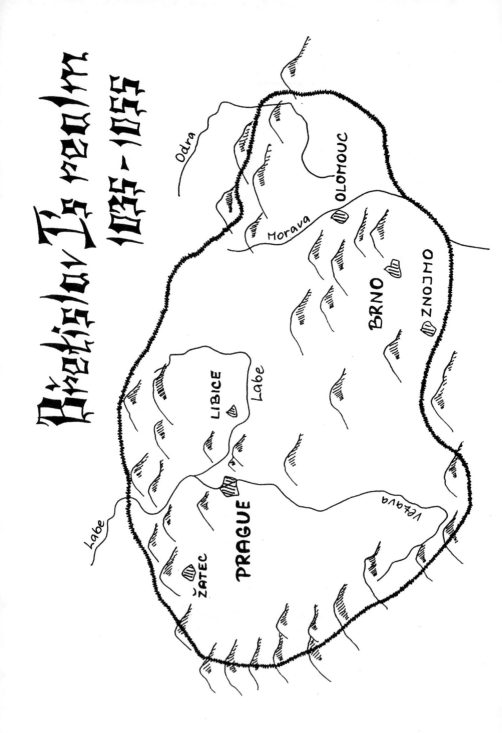

Břetislav I's realm
1035–1055

Odra

OLOMOUC

Morava

BRNO

ZNOJMO

LIBICE

Labe

Labe

ŽATEC

PRAGUE

Vltava

1012 - 1033
OLDŘICH,
brother of Boleslav III
and Jaromír,
Knight of Bohemia

Oldřich deprived his brother Jaromír of the reign over Bohemia, chased him out of the country, regained Moravia from Poland and entrusted its administration to his son Břetislav.

1033 - 1034
JAROMÍR,
brother of Boleslav III
and Oldřich,
Knight of Bohemia

Konrad II, King of Germany and emperor of Rome, imprisoned Oldřich, the Knight of Bohemia. A special expedition to Bohemia put through Jaromír's (third) appointment as Knight of Bohemia. Moravia remained under Břetislav's administration.

1034
OLDŘICH,
brother of Boleslav III
and Jaromír,
Knight of Bohemia

Back from prison, Oldřich acknowledged again as Czech sovereign (for the second time). He deprived his brother Jaromír of sight and imprisoned him.

1035 - 1055
BŘETISLAV I,
son of Oldřich,
Knight of Bohemia

Břetislav I, the new Knight of Bohemia, subjected part of Poland and Silesia. He resisted Heinrich III, King of Germany, surrendered eventually and took oath of fidelity. Together with Heinrich III, he took part in military expeditions to Hungary. On basis of negotiations he returned Kazimierz I, Polish Knight, Polish teritories and Silesia. Polish sovereign obliged himself to pay the Czechs a regular annual tribute. Břetislav I established Brno, Olomouc and Znojmo domains.

1040 Henry III's defeat at Brůdek, not far away from Domažlice.

1054 Quedlinburg's peace contract.

1054 Eldest Premyslide Succession Act, the so-called Seniorate.

15

Romance Style

Rotunda upon the hill of Řip

1055 - 1061 SPYTIHNĚV II, son of Břetislav I, Knight of Bohemia	Spytihněv II imprisoned about three hundred Moravian barons to bring Moravia closer to Bohemia. Pope entitled him to bear bishop's mitre.	1055 - 1057 Slav-ritual monks chased out of Sázava monastery. Monks left for Hungary.
1061 - 1092 VRATISLAV II, brother of Spytihněv II, Knight, since 1085 King of Bohemia	1081 - 1084 Czech forces participated in Roman cavalcade of Heinrich IV, King of Germany, to Italy. For the aid in the investiture battle, not far away from Rome, Heinrich IV, the newly inaugurated emperor, bestowed upon Vratislav II, the Czech sovereign, 1085 the royal crown, referring to his person only. Temporary, Vratislav II gained the teritory of Upper Lužice and part of eastern Moravia.	1063 Diocese of Olomouc founded. Slav monks recalled to Sázava monastery.
1092 KONRÁD I of BRNO, brother of Vratislav II, Knight of Bohemia	Konrád I of Brno had quite a short reign. Out of Vratislav II's sons, four held the sway: Břetislav, Bořivoj, Vladislav and Soběslav.	
1092 - 1100 BŘETISLAV II, son of Vratislav II, Knight of Bohemia	In the course of Břetislav II's reign Czech forces repeatedly attacked Silesia. The Polish, on their part were penetrating into Moravia. Vladislav Heřman, the Polish sovereign, made peace with Břetislav II and obliged himself to pay the tribute set up by Quedlinburg Peace Treaty of 1054.	Rest of paganism suppressed. 1096 - crusade to Palestine. Anti-Jew tumults in Bohemia.

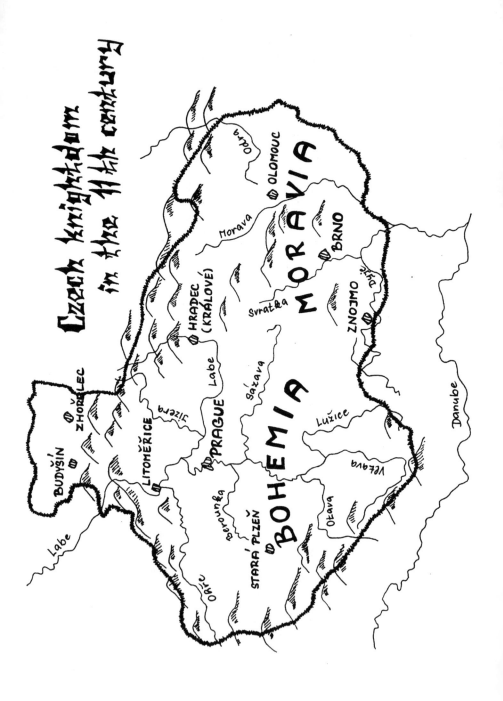

1101 - 1107 BOŘIVOJ II, brother of Břetislav II, Knight of Bohemia	Bořivoj II fighting for Polish throne. After promising ransom, Svatopluk, Knight of Olomouc, came back to Bohemia, supported by Boleslav III of Poland and Koloman of Hungary, to dethrone Bořivoj II.
1107 - 1109 SVATOPLUK of OLOMOUC, grandson of Břetislav I, Knight of Bohemia	Svatopluk undertook several invasions of Hungary. 1108, on knight Svatopluk's order, Czech peers of Vršovec massacred.
1109 - 1117 VLADISLAV I, brother of Bořivoj II, Knight of Bohemia	Invasion by Polish troops of Bohemia parried off by Vladislav I. 1114 Czech sovereign granted the dignity of the Imperial Butler. (In the 13th century the said dignity resulted in the right of Czech King to elect Emperor.)
1117 - 1120 BOŘIVOJ II, brother of Břetislav II, Knight of Bohemia	Bořivoj II called back from abroad to Bohemia by Vladislav I and enthroned (for the second time).
1120 - 1125 VLADISLAV I, brother of Bořivoj II, Knight of Bohemia	Vladislav I dethroned Bořivoj II and assumed reign (for the second time). Continuous disagreements between Premyslides. Prior to his death, Vladislav reconciled himself with Soběslav, his brother.
1125 - 1140 SOBĚSLAV I, brother of Vladislav I, Knight of Bohemia	In the wars with the Polish, Soběslav I reinforced the tribute set up by Peace Treaty of Quedlinburg in 1054. Put an end

1025 death of Cosmas, the Czech annalist.

1026 defeat of Lothar, the King of Germany, at Chlumec.

19

Vladislav II

to quarrels, disagreements and chaos in Bohemia caring for peace and improvement of his country.

1140 - 1172
VLADISLAV II,
son of Vladislav I,
Knight,
since 1158 King of Bohemia

Vladislav II participated in second crusade which, however, did not reach Palestine. After the failure, Czech sovereign returned via Constantinople and Kiev. In his absence, Soběslav, son of Soběslav I, tried to initiate a rebellion. He was, however, executed and imprisoned in Přimda. 1158 Vladislav II acquired from Friedrich I, German King and Roman Emperor, royal dignity for aid in expedition to Milano. Vladislav II renounced the throne in favour of his son Bedřich.

1147 The second crusade.

1158 Czechs in Milano.

1169 Erection of first stone bridge by Judith, Vladislav's spouse.

1172 - 1173
BEDŘICH I,
son of Vladislav II,
Knight of Bohemia

Bedřich I assumed reign in 1172. The Emperor Friedrich I bestowed royal insignia upon Oldřich, (younger son of Soběslav II) who, on his part, brought them over to Soběslav, better entitled for the dignity of knight of Bohemia.

1173 - 1178
SOBĚSLAV II,
son of Soběslav I,
Knight of Bohemia

After ascending to the throne, Soběslav II took people under his protection (hence Knight the Peasant). Thus, he lost both the nobility's and Emperor's favour. Friedrich the Emperor bestowed Bohemia as upon Bedřich, Knight of Bohemia, dethroned in 1173. Bedřich dethroned by military invasion and assumed reign for the second time.

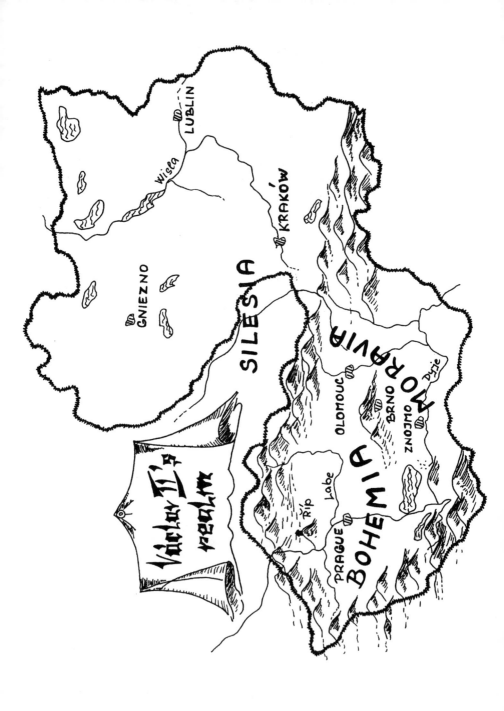

1178 - 1189 BEDŘICH I, son of Vladislav II, Knight of Bohemia	Bedřich I's reign dependent on Emperor of Rome. 1182 disconcerted nobility elected Konrád Ota of Znojmo as Knight of Bohemia. Bedřich I asked Emperor's assistance to settle the discrepancy in Regensburg so that Bedřich I remained Knight and Konrád Ota was given Moravia, the Bohemia-independent margraviate, as his feud. 1186 Bedřich's supremacy confirmed by Konrád Ota, Margrave of Moravia.	1186 Jindřich Břetislav, Bishop of Prague, proclaimed Imperial Knight.
1189 - 1191 KONRÁD II OTA, great-grandson of Břetislav I, Knight of Bohemia and Margrave of Moravia	Knight Konrád Ota's statutes (oldest code in Czech territories) issued. Konrád Ota took part in the military expedition of King Heinrich IV to Italy. He died in the course of this expedition.	1189 The third crusade.
1191 - 1192 VÁCLAV II brother of Soběslav II, Knight of Bohemia	Václav II's reign lasted half a year only. After Czech nobility's rebellion he was dethroned.	
1192 - 1193 PŘEMYSL OTAKAR I, son of Vladislav II, Knight of Bohemia	For participation in conspiracy against Heinrich IV, King of Germany and Emperor of Rome, Přemysl Otakar I dethroned. Both Bohemia and Moravia bestowed as feud upon Jindřich Břetislav, Bishop of Prague.	
1193 - 1197 JINDŘICH BŘETISLAV, cousin of Bedřich I, Knight of Bohemia and Margrave of Moravia	Jindřich Břetislav undertook a military expedition to Moravia to dethrone Margrave Vladislav, imprisoned later in Prague. Přemysl, still living abroad,	1195 Czech troops' invasion to Meisen.

Zvíkov

reconfirmed as Czech sovereign
by Emperor of Rome.

1197
VLADISLAV JINDŘICH,
son of Vladislav II,
Knight of Bohemia
and Margrave of Moravia

Vladislav Jindřich appointed
Daniel II as new Bishop of
Prague. Voluntarily renounced
the Czech throne in favor of his
brother Přemysl and subjected
himself as Margrave of Moravia.
This was the end of the second
turbulent era (following Vladislav II's resignation).

1197 - 1230
PŘEMYSL OTAKAR I,
son of Vladislav II,
King of Bohemia

1198 Přemysl Otakar I acquired,
in the disputes referring to the
German throne, hereditary royal
sovereignty both from Philipp
of Schwabenland and Otto IV,
his adversary. This sovereignty
was in 1204 confirmed by Inno-
centius III, Pope of Rome. 1212,
Friedrich II, new Emperor of
Rome, published Golden Charter
of Sicily. The king of Bohemia
was granted following privileges:
a) King of Germany does
not elect but confirms Czech
sovereign only,
b) crown heredity guar-
ranteed,
c) duty of providing 300
cavaliers for coronation trips to
Rome or, as recompense, 300
talents of silver,
d) King of Bohemia's du-
ty to participate in councils held
not far away from the Czech
frontier only,
e) privilege of electing
King of Rome,

Foundation of towns, defores-
tations, German colonization.

1216 Voidance of Seniorate set
up by Břetislav I in 1054.

	f) Moravia and diocese of Prague acknowledged as integral parts of Czech realm.	1226 Czechs invade Austria.
1230 - 1253 VÁCLAV I, son of Přemysl Otakar I, King of Bohemia	Václav I invited foreigners to Bohemia. 1246, Vladislav, the Dauphin, gained Austrian territories by marriage with Gertrud, heiress of Babenbergs (died in 1247). 1248 Přemysl the Dauphin at the head of rebellion against the King. Followed by a temporary reconciliation, power division took place both in Bohemia and Moravia. Přemysl retained the dignity of King Junior. 1251 Přemysl, Margrave of Moravia appointed Duke by Austrian nobility.	1241 Tatars' invasion of Hungary. Fortification of towns, erection of castles, introduction of chivalrous manners, organizing tournaments, colonization of boundary forests.
1253 - 1278 PŘEMYSL OTAKAR II, son of Václav I, King of Bohemia, King of Gold and Iron	1260 Přemysl Otakar II acquired Styria in the battle of Kresenbrun fought against Hungarian King Béla IV. 1266 he occupied Cheb area as marriage portion of his mother Kunhuta. 1269 he acquired Carinthia and Krein by treaty. 1276 he fought against the Roman King Rudolph I of Habsburg. After defeat he gave up Alpine territories, Austria and Cheb area and accepted Bohemian countries as feud. 1278 he died in the battle of Moravian Field.	
1278 - 1305 VÁCLAV II, son of Přemysl Otakar II, King of Bohemia and Poland	1278 - 1283 tutor reign of Václav's uncle Otto of Brandenburg who established imprisonment of Václav the Dauphin.	Spring 1282 - starvation in Bohemia.

1283 - 1288 tutor reign of Záviš of Falkenstein. After 1288 Václav II assumed reign, acquired part of Silesia, Kraków and Sandomer areas. 1300 coronated as King of Poland. 1301 acquired, for his son Václav, Hungarian crown (as King of Hungary, he assumed the name Ladislav V). 1304 Václav II's troops entered Hungary to help his son against nobility. In the same year, he warded off Albrecht of Austria's invasion of Bohemia.

1300 groszes of Prague (coins) of a constant silver valour minted.

1305 - 1306
VÁCLAV III,
son of Václav II,
King of Bohemia
and Hungary

Václav III renounced all claims associated with Hungarian crown. He was, however, about to keep Polish crown. In August 4th 1306 Václav III was assassinated in Olomouc during the course of his military expedition to Poland against Vladislav Lokietek. This is the death of the last Premyslide on Czech throne.

August 4th 1306, House of Premyslide ended by the sword, after more than 400 years of historic reign.

1306
JINDŘICH
KORUTANSKÝ,
(Spouse Anna,
daughter of Václav II)
King of Bohemia

Jindřich Korutanský proposed, as first, to assume the crown of Bohemia. In September 1306 he was elected King. In the meantime, Albrecht I, King of Rome, proclaimed the heritage of the House of Premyslides to be dead. Thus, he wished to reserve it for his son Rudolph. In October 1306 Rudolph was elected King of Bohemia.

Grosz of Prague,
after 1300 (reverse and obverse)

1306 - 1307
RUDOLPH
OF HABSBURG,
son of Roman King
Albrecht I,
King of Bohemia

Rudolph of Habsburg married Eliška, widow of Václav II, Czech nobility, however, denied the oath. In 1307 he died when on an expedition against Czech noblemen besieging Horažďovice.

1307 - 1310
JINDŘICH
KORUTANSKÝ,
(spouse Anna,
daughter of Václav II),
King of Bohemia

In 1307 Jindřich Korutanský was accepted, by most noblemen, to be King of Bohemia. Due to his indecision, the country fell into chaos. The nobility's resistance kept growing gradually. In 1310 Konrád, abbot of Zbraslav, reached an agreement regarding the marriage of the 14-year-old Jan, son of Roman King Heinrich IV of Luxemburg to the 18-year-old Eliška, daughter of Václav II. In 1310 Jindřich Korutanský chased out of the country (was exiled).

1310 - 1346
JAN LUCEMBURSKÝ,
son of Roman emperor
Heinrich VII,
King of Bohemia

1310 marriage of Jan Lucemburský with Eliška from the House of Premyslide. The country was administered by Peter of Aspelt, instead of the young king and, subsequently, by Jindřich z Lipé. The king himself left his country in search of adventures. Jan Lucemburský acquired further portions of Silesia, Budyšín area (Lužice), Zhořelec area, Cheb area indefinitely and part of Italy temporarily. In 1334 Karel the Dauphin was appointed Margrave of Moravia. In 1337 Karel accepted his father's final consent to govern the whole realm. 1346 Jan Lucemburský died in battle

1310 - 1314 Dalimil's Chronicle.

1315 Valdenship in Bohemia.

1328, 1337, 1344 Jan's crusades to Prussia.

1335 Trenčín Treaty.

1344 Diocese of Prague promoted to archdiocese; Arnošt z Pardubic.

Karel IV

of Crécy fought between the French and the English. Jan died on the French side.

**1346 - 1378
KAREL IV,
son of Jan Lucemburský,
King of Bohemia
and Emperor of Rome**

Karel ascended to the throne as the King of Rome. 1355 he acquired the title of the Emperor of Rome. He proved to be the most prominent sovereign of Europe in those days. Sponsor of arts, literature, architecture and the Church. He was a distinguished politician; he earned merit through territorial growth of Czech state, strengthened by its independence on German realm, which provided for economic boom of the country. In 1349 margraviate of Moravia governed by independent hegemony of a minor line of the House of Luxembourg. Majestas Carolina, the land's code, was presented to the Assembly of deputies but was rejected by the nobility. In 1356 the Golden Charter of Karel IV provided, among other things, for the election of German kings by the majority of Electors, the first place being reserved for the King of Bohemia. Electors were recommended to have their sons taught in Czech. 1361-1362 rose a strong military coalition of the Polish and Hungarian Kings, the Duke of Austria, the Count of Tyrol and others against Karel IV. Owing to Karel's diplomatic skills, this union disintegrated without causing any grave damages to Czech territories. In 1363 Václav IV, son of Karel IV, coronated as King of Bohemia. In 1364 Karel IV and Rudolph IV,

1347 Foundation of Monastery na Slovanech intended for Slav monks.

1348 Foundation of Prague University.

Autumn 1348 Bohemia and Moravia struck by plague devastating all of Evrope.

Foundation of the New City of Prague. Construction of Saint Vitus's Cathedral started (Mathew of Arras and Petr Parléř). Edification of Karlštejn castle.

Constructions of cathedrals, monasteries, castles: golden era of arts.

1357 Construction of Stone Bridge over Vltava River in Prague started (Petr Parléř).

1363 Konrad Waldhauser started his preaching activities in Prague. Rectifying movement started in Bohemia.

60's - 70's of 14th century - first complete translation of Bible.

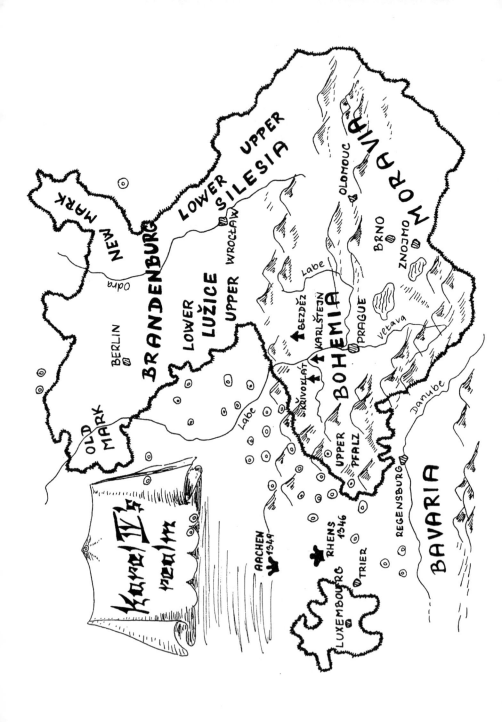

Duke of Austria concluded hereditary contracts between the House of Luxembourg and the House of Habsburg. 1376 Karel's son Václav IV elected King of Rome. In the course of his reign Karel IV confirmed privileges of the realm of Bohemia, issued Acts on perpetual annexation of Moravia, Silesia and Upper Lužice to Bohemia. Through marriage, he acquired last Silesian principalities, bought and annexed Lower Lužice, subjected Brandenburg territory, bought Upper Pfalz and other German territories. Thus, the Czech crown became the largest political formation of Central Europe. In his last will, Karel IV divided his lands among his sons; Václav IV was to reign in Bohemia, Silesia, Budyšín area and Lower Lužice and become the feudal lord of Moravia, the Opava area and of imperial feuds respectively. Zikmund was to obtain most of the Brandenburg area and be vested with electorial rights. Jan was to get Zhořelec area and the rest of the Brandenburg area. After the death of Karel IV's stepbrother Václav Luxemburg area fell to the share of Václav IV. In his lifetime, Karel IV was married four times. His first wife was Blanka, Princess of France of the House of Valois. After her death he married Anna of Pfalz, daughter of Rudolph II of Pfalz, one of his gravest adversaries. His third wife was Anna Svídnická, heiress of the last principalities of Silesia, which was, in those days, not yet

1374 Jan Milíč z Kroměříže died in Avignon.

35

Jan Hus

annexed to Czech kingdom. For the fourth time Karel IV married Elisabeth of Pommern, granddaughter of King of Poland, famous for her strength. In November 1378 Karel IV died.

1378 - 1419
VÁCLAV IV,
son of Karel IV,
King of Bohemia
and King of Rome

Václav IV, then 18 years old, assumed the reign in Bohemia and in the Roman empire. In those days, struggles with higher nobility broke out. Václav IV rejected Roman cavalary and imperial crown. In 1394 Václav was captured by the Unity of Barons led by Jošt, Margrave of Moravia and Ota of Bergov, supreme Purgrave of Prague. Conciliation was mediated by Jan Zhořelecký. In 1394 the war between Václav IV and the Czech barons ended through an armistice. 1400 Václav IV dethroned by Rhine Electors. 1402 - 1403 King captured for the second time by the Unity of Barons led by Zikmund Lucemburský, and temporarily imprisoned in Vienna. Zikmund Lucemburský appointed by Václav IV as regent of the Czech kingdom. In 1409 Václav IV issued the Edict of Kutná Hora altering University voting ratio so that the Czechs acquired three and the rest of nations (Poles, Saxons and Bavarians) one vote each. German Masters and students left Prague. In 1411 Zikmund Lucemburský was appointed the King of Rome. In 1419 town councillors thrown out of New Town Hall windows. In 1419 Václav IV died.

Summer 1380 plague epidemic in Bohemia.

1389 Jewish holocaust in Prague.

1391 Foundation of Chapel of Bethlehem.

1393 Jan z Pomuku drowned in Vltava (Jan Nepomucký).

Matěj z Janova and Tomáš ze Štítného active in reformatory movement.

1402 Jan Hus preacher in the Chapel of Bethlehem.

1412 Hus's controversies with Church as regards indulgences.

1414 Calix communion.

July 6, 1415 Master Jan Hus burnt at the stake in Constance.

1416 Jeroným Pražský burnt at the stake in Constance.

Jan Žižka z Trocnova

1419 - 1434
HUSSITE WARS' ERA

The number of adherents to Hus's doctrine in Bohemia increased quickly. Tension between Hussite inhabitants and Catholic nobility culminated. In 1420 Pope Martin declared crusade against the Czechs. In April 1420 Zikmund Lucemburský, King of Rome and of Hungary, marched to Prague. Hussite leader Jan Žižka z Trocnova united with Praguers on the basis of Four Prague Articles, i. e.:
1) free preaching of God's Word,
2) Utraquist communion,
3) clergy to drop secular reigning,
4) mortal sins to be punished.

In 1420 Prague besieged by crusaders, Zikmund Lucemburský let himself be coronated King of Bohemia, however he was not accepted by the majority of nation. After the death of Miluláš z Husi, the Captain Jan Žižka set himself at the head of Taborites. In 1421, the Congress of Tábor held with the first participation of royal towns. The Congress established government of 20 land regents. Zikmund Lucemburský deprived of Czech throne. After that, crown offered to the Knight of Lithuania Vitold, brother of the King of Poland. In August 1422, the second congress held in Čáslav, where Zikmund Korybut, nephew of King of Poland and the Archduke of Lithuania was accepted as the sovereign of Bohemia. In December 1422, Korybut was removed by his uncle Vitold. 1423 Zikmund

1420 First Crusade to Bohemia.

1420 Battle at Sudoměř and Vítkov. First Hussites's victories over royal chivalry.

1420 Battle at Vyšehrad. Praguers beat troops of Zikmund Lucemburský.

1421 Second crusade to Bohemia. Crusaders taking to flight.

1422 Battle at Německý Brod; Zikmund Lucemburský defeated.

1422 Jan Želivský executed treacherously.

1422 Third crusade to Bohemia, coming back.

1422 Hussite chronicle by Vavřinec z Březové.

1423 Žižka's Military Order.

Gothics
St. Vitus's Cathedral at Prague Castle

Lucemburský gave Albrecht V, his son-in-law and Duke of Austria, Moravia as feud and appointed him as heir to the Czech crown. In 1424 Zikmund Korybut returned, mediated an armistice between Jan Žižka and Praguerites, assisted by Jan Rokycana, in the field of Špitál. 1427 - 1433, the so-called graceful rides, i. e. Hussite troops expeditions (those of Prague, Tábor and the Orpans') to surrounding countries, took place. Graceful rides were expected to make the enemy negotiate. In 1429 there was a meeting of Zikmund Lucemburský with Hussites' representatives, particularly Prokop Holý and Merhart z Hradce. It was to reconciliate Hussites with Church. The meeting resulted in failure. In 1432 negotiations between Hussites and messengers of Congress of Basle held to enable the former freely to defend their doctrine on both the biblical basis and the behaviour of the early Church. The results of these negotiations are summarized in the so-called Cheb Judge. In 1433 the Hussites led by Prokop Holý participated in the Congress of Basle. The negotiations continued in Prague. In 1435 new negotiations opened with Zikmund. In 1436 the Congress of Jihlava proclaimed (issued) Compactates setting up Convention between the Congress of Basle and the Hussites of Bohemia and introduced utraquism in Bohemia.

1423 Battle at Hořice. Žižka beat the troops led by Čeněk z Vartenberka.

1424 Death of Jan Žižka z Trocnova.

1426 Battle at Ústí nad Labem. Crusaders beaten by Hussites of Prokop Holý.

1427 Fourth Crusade to Bohemia.

1427 Battle at Tachov. Crusaders' flight.

1431 Fifth Crusade to Bohemia.

1431 Battle at Domažlice. Immense army of crusaders from all of Europe fled from Hussites.

1434 Battle at Lipany. United nobility beat Taborites and Orphans led by Prokop Holý. Prokop Holý, called the Great, fell in the battle.

1436 - 1437
ZIKMUND
LUCEMBURSKÝ,
brother of Václav IV,
King of Bohemia
and Hungary,
Emperor of Rome

Though coronated as King of Bohemia in 1420, Zikmund Lucemburský did not reign. As a matter of fact, in 1436 he was accepted by the Hussite estates as King of Bohemia after granting them several privileges. In 1437 Zikmund Lucemburský died while leaving Prague.

1437 Jan Roháč z Dubé executed.

1437 - 1439
ALBRECHT II
of HABSBURG,
son-in-law of Zikmund
Lucemburský,
King of Bohemia,
Hungary and Rome

The part of the nobility held by Oldřich z Rožmberka and Merhart z Hradce elected Albrecht II as the King of Bohemia. The party of Hynek Ptáček z Pirkštejna, together with the Hussite nobility, preferred Kazimierz, brother of Vladislav III, the King of Poland. A conspiracy was broken out against Albrecht, but it was suppressed. Albrecht II of Habsburg died returning from an unsuccessful expedition to Hungaria against the Turks.

1439 Plague epidemic in Bohemia.

1439 - 1452
INTERREGNUM

In 1440 Hynek Ptáček z Pirkštejna was elected Chieftain of four East-Bohemian regions. In 1444 the Provincial Congress acknowledged claims of the four-year-old Ladislav Pohrobek, son of Albrecht of Habsburg in regards to the Czech throne. In 1444 the twenty-four-year-old Jiří z Poděbrad became his successor. Jiří's party became Unity in Kutná Hora. 1448 Jiří z Poděbrad conquered Prague. Since then, he vested the sovereignty of the Regent of the Czech kingdom. In 1449 Party

CZECH STATE in the course of rule of Poděbrady's reign 1458-1471

countries occupied by M. Korvín [1468-1478]

PRUSSIA
Odra
Labe
POLAND
SAXONY
UPPER LUŽICE
LOWER LUŽICE
SILESIA
Odra
Visla
BOHEMIA
CHEB
PRAGUE
PODĚBRADY
TÁBOR
Vltava
MORAVIA
Morava
Danube
BAVARIA
Inn
AUSTRIA
SPIŠ
Tisa
Váh
BRATISLAVA
HUNGARY
Tisa

1452 - 1453 JIŘÍ Z PODĚBRAD, Regent of Czech kingdom	of Jindřich z Rožmberka established as the Unity of Strakonice. In 1452 the Congress of Prague represented by adherents of the Party of Strakonice and Poděbrady, appointed Jiří z Poděbrad to be Regent.	
1453 - 1457 LADISLAV POHROBEK, son of Albrecht II of Habsburg, King of Bohemia and Hungary	Following Ladislav Pohrobek's coronation, the position of Jiří z Poděbrad remained unchanged. In 1453 the renovation of Provincial Court contributed significantly to strengthening judicial order of the country. King Ladislav Pohrobek died at the age of seventeen, prior to his marriage with Magdalene, Princess of France.	1453 Constantinople conquered by the Turks.
1458 - 1471 JIŘÍ Z PODĚBRAD, King of Bohemia	In 1458 Jiří z Poděbrad was coronated as the King of Bohemia. He subjected Moravia and Silesia. In 1465 the Catholic nobility established the anti-royal Unity of Zelená Hora. Matyáš Korvín, King of Hungary, son-in-law of Jiří z Poděbrad declared war on the Czechs in 1468 and started a crusade. He was beaten by Jiří z Poděbrad's troops. In 1469 the Catholic nobility elected Matyáš as the King of Bohemia. The election took place in Olomouc. Czech Congress refused the Olomouc election of Matyáš and confirmed right of succession for the sake of Vladislav Jagelonský, son of Kazimier, King of Poland.	1457 Foundation of Brethren's Unity in Kunvald. 1460 death of Petr Chelčický. 1462 Pope Pius II cancelled Compactates of Basle. 1466 Pope Pius II proclaimed crusade against Czechs. 1471 Death of Jan z Rokycan, Archbishop of Prague (not confirmed by Papal Court).

Rennaissance

Queen Ann's Summer - mansion at Prague Castle (Belvedere)

**1471 - 1516
VLADISLAV II
JAGELONSKÝ,
King of Bohemia
and Hungary**

1471 Vladislav Jagelonský coronated King of Bohemia. Catholic nobility, however, maintained acknowledgement of Matyáš Korvín. The latter, reigning, in those days, over a part of Bohemia, half of Moravia, Silesia and Lužice, let himself be coronated by Pope's Legate as King of Bohemia in Jihlava and started struggling with Vladislav. 1476 armistice proclaimed in Olomouc. Both sovereigns were to be vested with title King of Bohemia. While Vladislav reigned in Bohemia only, Matyáš's reign comprised by-territories of the Crown, Moravia, Silesia and Lužice respectively. Thus, Czech Crown was split in two parts. 1490 after Matyáš's death, Czech Crown reintegrated. In the same year, Vladislav II Jagelonský elected King of Hungary. 1509 Ludvík, son of Vladislav, coronated King of Bohemia. 1515 King Vladislav II concluded a Succession Treaty comprising material unions of his children with Habsburgs.

1483 Prague tumults.

1483 Plague in Bohemia.

1485 Congress of Kutná Hora; religious armistice between Catholic and Caliciste nobilities.

1497 Resolution on turning over serfs to previous lords.

1500 Provincial statuses strengthen nobility's power on detriment of towns.

**1516 - 1526
LUDVÍK JAGELONSKÝ,
son of Vladislav II
Jagelonský,
King of Bohemia
and Hungary**

After death of Vladislav II Jagelonský, Ludvík Jagelonský, his eleven-year-old son, ascended to the throne; Lord of Rožmitál was the Regent. The young King resided in Buda, not having any chance to interfere wirh the course of Czech events. 1526 a threat of a repeated Turkish invasion to Hungary. Ludvík Jagelonský faced enemy at the head of very small army.

1517 both the nobility and the townspeople united through St. Václav's Treaty. The towns keeping participation in the Congress, the nobility granted the privilege of brewing beer. Nobility and townspeople were reconciliated.

1519 Presentation of Martin Luther's adherents in Prague. Adherents of Calix started dividing into neo- and old utraquists.

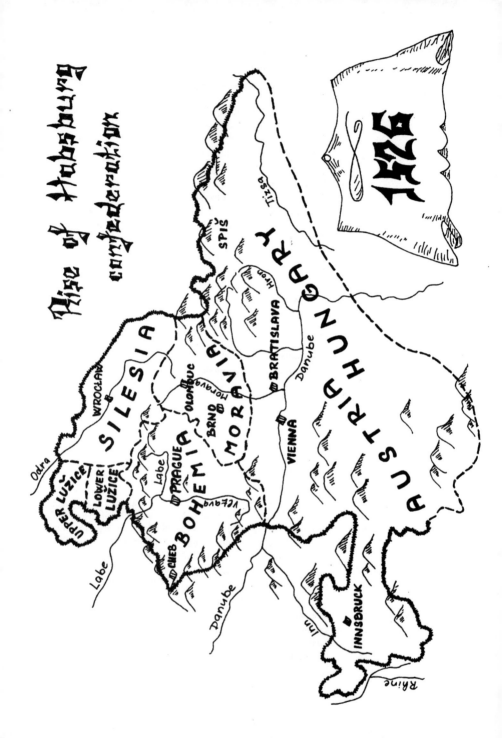

Rise of Habsburg confederation

1526

In the fatal battle at Mainz in South Hungary his troops sufferred a bitter defeat by the Turks. The twenty-year-old King perished in flight. In his person, the branch of Czech Jagellons died out. A few candidates took interest in the vacant throne.

1524 Upheaval in Prague. Pašek's Calicist party assumed reign in Prague. Havlas's Luther's party suppressed.

1526 - 1564
FERDINAND I
of HABSBURG,
grandson of Maximilian I
(Roman Emperor),
King of Bohemia
and Hungary,
Emperor of Rome

Provincial Congress elected Ferdinand of Habsburg, Archduke of Austria, the new sovereign. He acquired also Crown of Hungary. Nobody could then forsee Czech, Austrian and Hungarian territories to remain under sovereignty of the House of Habsburg for as long as 400 years' time. 1527 Ferdinand I of Habsburg coronated King of Bohemia. In the same year, central court authorities established in Vienna with Czech Chamber subordinated. 1531 Ferdinand I of Habsburg elected King of Rome. 1547 due to failure of Catholic Statuses' rebellion, towns lost a part of their privileges. 1548 Court of Appeal, as appealing instance of towns' courts, established. 1556 Ferdinand I elected Emperor of Rome.

1528 Religious disputes.

1527 The Turks in Vienna.

1547 "Bloody Congress"

Mandates issued against Brethrens' Union.

1556 Jezuits introduced in Bohemia.

1561 Archbishop's stool of Prague reoccupied by Antonín Brus z Mohelnice after more than a century's break.

1564 Calix's reapproval.

1555 Peace of Augsburg guaranteeing religious freedom to Protestant statuses. "He who owns the territory owns the faith" set up as principle. (Subjects were to confess their lordship's religion, or go.)

1564 - 1576
MAXIMILIAN II,
son of Ferdinand I,
King of Bohemia
and Hungary,
Emperor of Rome

Maximilian II was a mild and tolerant sovereign, however fearing the Pope, he did not wish religious liberty on proper territories. 1575 Maximilian II approved orally of the so-called Czech confession, i.e. agreement of Czech non-Catholics on reli-

1571 Death of Jan Blahoslav, Bishop of Brethrens' Unity.

1573 Foundation of Olomouc University.

Rudolph II

gious matters. The main principle consisted of the fact that subjects needn't be of the same confession as their lords.

1576 - 1611
RUDOLPH II,
son of Maximilian II,
King of Bohemia
and Hungary,
Emperor of Rome

Rudolph II chose Prague as his residence. His court became a brilliant European centre of Arts and Science. In the course of his reign counter-reformation started openly. 1599 non-Catholic servants removed from the Czech Office, by then the supreme authority of the Czech Kingdom. 1602 Mandate against Brethrens' Unity renewed. 1608 Moravians assisted by Matthias threw off Catholic administration of the country and elected Karel Senior of Žerotín, Provincial Captain. Moravian troops join Matthias marching towards Prague. Matthias was to make his brother give up his throne. Czech Congress took advantage of the straits and extorted promise of fast settling of major political and religious requirements. Matthias's expedition into Prague proved to be a success. Rudolph II receded fully. By Libeň treaty, he passed his reign over Hungary, Austria and Moravia to Matthias who was, at the same time, accepted as the future King of Bohemia. For support proved, the sovereign was compelled to issue to Czech statuses 1609 the so-called Rudolph's Majestate confirming Czech confession. Following that, a 30-member corps of non-catholic faith defenders was established Ru-

"Golden Age" of Czech literature.

Danial Adam z Veleslavína.

1579 - 1594 Bible of Kralice, a six-volume, by-lined translation of biblical text into Czech language, issued under sponsorship of Brethrens' Unity.

Activities of Tycho de Brahe and Jan Kepler, the astrologers, Bartholomew Spranger, Hans von Aachen, Giuseppe Arcimboldo, the engraver, Jiljí Sadeler, the sculptor, Adrian de Vries, the sculptor, and the like.

Rudolph's Gallery becomes known world-wide.

1584 Gregorian calender introduced in Bohemia and Moravia.

1584 - 1590 Jakub Krčín z Jelčan founds Rožmberk, the largest Czech pond.

1594 First blast-iron furnace erected in Bohemia (Dvůr Králové u Berouna).

Habsburg confederation in the second half of the 16th century

TRANSYLVANIA

HUNGARY

UZHGOROD
BANSKÁ ŠTIAVNICA
PEST
BUDA
Danube

SILESIA

MORAVIA
BRNO

BOHEMIA
PRAGUE
Labe
LUŽICE
UPPER LOWER
CHEB AREA

LOWER AUSTRIA
VIENNA
UPPER AUSTRIA

STEIERMARK
GRAZ

KÄRNTEN

KRAIN
ZAGREB
CROATIA

BOSNIA

ISTRA

INN
Danube
BREGENZERLAND
INNSBRUCK
TIROL

ADRIATIC SEA

dolph II tried to alter the given status quo intending to bring about an anti-status upheaval and foil Matthias's successorship. This was supported by Passau's Electors, invading Bohemia in 1611. The latter were chased by Statuses. In the same year Rudolph II gave up Czech Crown, keeping only the dignity of Emperor of the Saint Roman Realm. Soon thereafter he died. This was the last Habsburg sovereign residing in Prague.

1600 Jan Jesenský - Jessenius performed in public first anatomical dissection in Prague.

1611 - 1619
MATTHIAS,
brother of Rudolph II,
King of Bohemia
and Hungary,
Emperor of Rome

1611 Matthias ascended to Czech throne. After Rudolph's death he was granted the title of Roman Emperor. As a politician of a milder sort, he tried to avoid controversies with Czech statutes. 1615 Provincial Congress proclaimed the Czech language to be the only legitimate language of Congress and other official negotiations. 1617 Catholic part of nobility present at the Congress put through acknowledgement of Ferdinand of Styriz as future King of Bohemia. Opposition of Statuses reacted to Majestate's violation by throwing Martinic and Slavata, Habsburg governors and Fabricius, the scribe, out the windows of Prague Castle. Then, the government composed of 30 directors was elected. The same started, without delay, hiring military troops and asking for help abroad. This was the beginning of Czech Statutes Rebellion and, consequently, of the Thirty Years' War.

Protestants' oppression.

1618 Prague defenstration.

1618 - 1648 Thirty Years' War.

Ferdinand II

1619 FERDINAND II cousin of Matthias, King of Bohemia, Hungary and Rome	Rebellion against the King spread over all territories of Czech Crown. July 31, 1619 General Assembly of Prague approved of the new Constitution. Czech Kingdom changed into Confederation of countries with equal rights and sovereign eligible. August 19, 1619 Ferdinand II deprived of Czech throne by General Assembly.	1592 - 1670 Jan Amos Komenský (Comenius). 1619 Ferdinand II of Habsburg elected Emperor of Rome.
1619 - 1620 FRIEDRICH VON DER PFALZ, King of Bohemia (Hibernal King)	Congress elected Friedrich von der Pfalz to be the new King of Bohemia. Directors' Government replaced by the renewed Corps of Supreme provincial Servants elected from nobility only. In September 1620, imperial and leagistic troops started an expedition to Prague. November 8, 1620 historical battle on Bílá Hora (White Mountain) resulted in Statuses' defeat. Friedrich von der Pfalz retired to Silesia. Prague surrenders together with most Czech towns without fighting. Moravia occupied without resistence. Later so did Lower Lužice, Silesia and Upper Lužice. Friedrich von der Pfalz left for Netherlands. Up to his death in 1632 he considered himself to be King of Bohemia without stepping on Czech soil anymore.	1620 Battle on Bílá Hora (White Mountain).
1620 - 1637 FERDINAND II, cousin of Matthias, King of Bohemia and Hungary, Emperor of Rome	The territories of Czech Crown resubjected to the Emperor. New Constitution was a hard blow for Statuses and the country. So was the renewed provincial administration in Bohemia 1627	

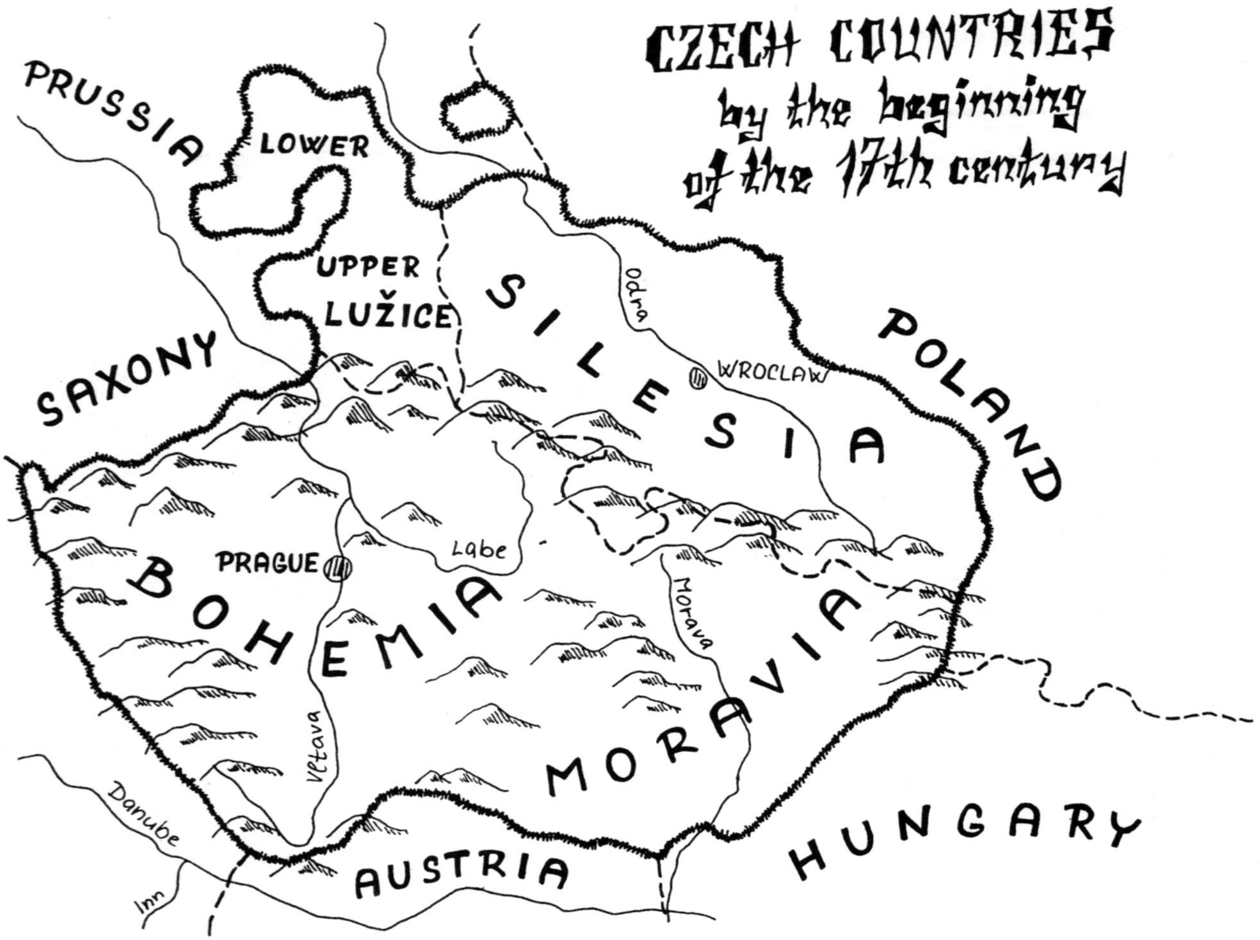

CZECH COUNTRIES by the beginning of the 17th century

POLAND

HUNGARY

SILESIA

WROCLAW

Odra

Morava

MORAVIA

UPPER LUŽICE

Labe

AUSTRIA

LOWER

PRUSSIA

BOHEMIA

PRAGUE

Vltava

SAXONY

Danube

Inn

and in Moravia in 1628. In the House of Habsburg, Czech Crown became hereditary also on the destaff side, the Czech language made equal with the German. Position of towns in Provincial Congress restricted. Catholic confession was the only one permitted. As a consequence, tens of thousands of people abandoned their country not to be obliged to give up their confession. 1630 Saxons besieged Prague. Protestants' rights renewed in those days. 1632 Albrecht of Waldstein, whose power in Bohemia culminated, invaded Prague. After, Waldstein started clandestine negotiations with the Swedes and non-Catholic refugees. 1634 Waldstein's assassination in Cheb. His enormous property confiscated. 1635 Ferdinand II gave up, on approval of the Statuses, both territories of Lužice in favour of Saxony. Thus, these territories remained separated from Czech Crown for as long as two and a half centuries.

June 21, 1621 twenty-seven leaders of Czech rebellion executed in Old-Town Square Prague. Among the victims were 3 lords (Kryštof Harant z Polžic a Bezdružic, Václav Budovec z Budova and Jáchym Ondřej Šlik), 7 knights and 17 townsmen.

Confiscation, Counter-Reformation, emigration.

1622 Charles University entrusted to Jesuites.

1634 - 1648 The Swedes in Moravia several times.

1637 - 1657
FERDINAND III,
son of Ferdinand II,
King of Bohemia
and Hungary,
Emperor of Rome

Ferdinand III issued "Declaratories" alleviating Czech administration. The signing of Peace of Westphalia on October 24, 1648 frustrated hopes of Habsburgs to dominate Europe. There was a disastrous result of the Thirty Years' War. Number of inhabitants on Czech territories sank from between one quarter to one third to 1 - 1.1 million in Bohemia, 0.5 - 0.6 million in

1610 - 1674 Karel Škréta, Czech painter.

1654 Four Faculties united in Charles-Ferdinand University and vested with new administration.

1653 - 1656 "tax rules", Enlistment of all subjects; settlements and townspeople's houses in the country.

57

CZECH COUNTRIES after lost of LUŽICE in 1635

SILESIA

MORAVIA

BOHEMIA

WROCŁAW

PRAGUE

Odra

Odra

Morava

Labe

Labe

Vltava

Moravia and 1 million in Silesia respectively. In Bohemia alone, contemporary sources refer to 270 devastated castles, over 100 towns and 1100 villages. Gradual restoration of order after Peace of Westphalia, Counter-Reformation, however, continued. 1646 coronation of Ferdinand IV, son of Emperor, and his premature death in 1654.

1653 - 1726 Erection of Clementinum, Jesuits' Hostel in Prague.

1657 - 1705
LEOPOLD I
son of Ferdinand III,
King of Bohemia
and Hungary,
Emperor of Rome

Sovereign's power getting absolute and centralized on all territories. Counter-Reformation alleviated to a trifle. 1679 - 1680 Big Rebellion of Peasantry in Bohemia. The rebellion started with petitions addressed to the Emperor and changed, later on, in an open fight. On March 22, 1680 a mandate confirming rights of the authorities as regards subjects, issued. The mandate made it impossible for a subject to address Emperor petitions which should, since then, be directed to regional captains only. It made void, simultaneously, all of subjects' privileges dating from the period prior to 1618, provided that they had not been confirmed by the authorities. The subjects' rebellion gradually assumed more radical aspects. On June 28, 1680, Leopold I issued his Manorial Patent which proved to be, in itself, a document of extraordinary importance delimitating correlations between authorities and subjects for centuries to come. Manorial

1663 - 1664 War with the Turks.

1663 The Turks plunder Moravia.

1679 - 1680 Plague on Czech territories.

1683 Vienna besieged by the Turks and their retreat.

First manufactures in Bohemia. Production of textiles.

1695 Jan Sladký Kozina executed in Plzeň (Pilsen).

1700 - 1714 Spanish heritage struggle. Habsburg monarchy became European power.

Baroque and Rococo
The Church of St. Nicholas in the Lesser Town of Prague

liabilities set for 3 days a week maximum, nobility may not levy illegal taxes, increase contributions and compel peasantry to buy overcharged produce. Prohibition of corporal punishment.

1705 - 1711
JOSEPH I
son of Leopold I,
King of Bohemia
and Hungary,
Emperor of Rome

1708 King of Bohemia's readmission to Corps of Electors. Following Thirty Years' War, the Habsburgs, as Kings of Bohemia, kept the right of election, but could not however, participate in meetings of Electors' Corps. This fact led to quite a dangerous preponderance of Protestant knights in Imperial Congress. Therefore Joseph I put through participation of a representative of the King of Bohemia in Electors' meetings. Under the influence of Eugene Savoy attitudes of Goverment of Vienna regarding individual territories of the monarchy start changing. National administration was to be provided by trained Servants taking in to account not only the sovereign's but also the Statuses' suggestions. 1710 Commission for Control of Renewed Provincial Establishment founded. Premature death of the Emperor ended the projects.

1705 - 1707 farmers' tumults in Upper Silesia.

1705 - 1714 Charles's Bridge in Prague adorned with sculptures by Ferdinand Maxmilian Brokoff and Matthias Bernard Braun.

1711 - 1740
KARL VI,
brother of Joseph I,
King of Bohemia
and Hungary,
Emperor of Rome

After years of struggles, Karl VI put an end to Spanish heriditary war with France. Thus, he gave up Spanish throne indefinitely. As compensation, however, Habsburg monarchy acquired North-Italian provinces, Naples

New favours for Jesuites; new patents against non-Catholics; quite a severe book censorship-Konias.

1713 - 1714 Last plague epidemic in Bohemia and Moravia.

61

Maria Theresia

area, Sardinia and Spanish Netherlands (Belgium). Karl VI, as the last living male Habsburg, was compelled to proclaim the so-called Pragmatic Sanction approved by Statutes in 1720, providing for both the integrity of Habsburg lands and successionship of Habsburg daughters should the male line die out. Though the Pragmatic Sanction was accepted by most European countries, still it did not prevent Austrian Heriditary War to break out after Karl VI's death. Habsburg male line died out.

1719 Matthias Bernard Braun, the sculptor, founded a unique Arts Gallery in east-Bohemian Kuks, presenting Virtues and Vices. Baroque in Bohemia.

1724 Beginnings of a stable Opera-House in Bohemia. Count Špork engaged Italian Opera Company to Prague and Kuks.

1668 - 1735 Petr Brandl, Czech painter.

Beginning of highway network construction with solid surface in Bohemia.

1740 - 1780
MARIA THERESIA,
daughter of Karl VI,
Queen of Bohemia
and Hungary,
Empress of Rome

1740 - 1748 Outbreak of Austrian Hereditary War. Maria Theresia has to defend the throne against countries which did not acknowledge her heriditary claims (particularly Prussia, Saxony, Bavaria and France). In wars she lost Kladsko and most of Silesia except Jeseník area, Opava area and Těšín area. The torn off territories annexed to Prussia.

1740 - 1742 First Silesian War.

1741
KARL ALBRECHT
of Bavaria

1741 Bavarian-French and Saxon troops occupy Prague. Karl Albrecht of Bavaria proclaimed himself King of Bohemia in Prague. Still, he left Prague in the same year and went to German realm. 1742 elected Emperor of Rome as Karl VII.

1743 Maria Theresia coronated in Prague as Queen of Bohemia, enjoying support of most of Czech nobility. 1745 after death of Karl VII of Bavaria, his son gave up his claims as regards

CZECH COUNTRIES after loss of SILESIA in 1742

TĚŠÍN AREA

OPAVA AREA

Odra

Morava

SILESIA

MORAVIA

BOHEMIA

Labe

Labe

Vltava

PRAGUE

Austrian heritage, confirmed Pragmatic Sanction and promised to give his voice for Franc of Lotharingia, spouse of Maria Theresia, to be elected Emperor. 1745 Franc of Lotharingia elected Emperor of Rome under the name Franc I. Since 1745 Maria Theresia was involved in hereditary war against France and Spain, finished in 1748 by Peace of Aachen. Maria Theresia lost a part of her provinces, acquired, however, general acknowled-gement of Pragmatic Sanction. The War reflected necessity of profound reforms of Habsburg monarchy. 1748 Provincial Deputations for Bohemia and Moravia established. These authorities were to introduce a new tax-levying system. 1749 Supreme Judicial Court in Vienna for individual provincial courts established. At the same time, Directorium for Public and Cameral Affairs set up. This new central office replaced previous Czech and Austrian Court Office. At Directorium's head stood the Silesian nobleman Friedrich Wilhelm Haugvic, promoter of Theresian reforms. 1749 Cancellation of Czech Royal Vice-Governor's Office in Prague and Provincial Government in Moravia. Both of them replaced by above-mentioned Deputations established in the past year. They assumed the name Royal Representations and Chamber. 1748 - 1751 Nationalization of District authorities.

1744 Jews expelled from Bohemia. This provision taken back after 4 year's time.

1744 - 1745 Second Silesian War, ended by Peace of Dresden made between Austria, Saxonia and Prussia.

Since 1745 continuation of Austrian hereditary war held in Western Europe and Italy.

1748 - 1757 Land-register of Maria Theresia replaced "tax-rule" and field registers. Lists of civic houses, farms and soil set up.

Care for education.

1750 Introduction of new unitary currency in all Habsburg lands. The Viennese marc of silver equals 12 tolers or 24 ducats.

Křivoklát

District captains, up to then status dignitaries, became government-paid officials. This meant Statuses' limitation. 1752 Custom's Duty Order for Czech territories protecting Czech production against imports, issued. 1753 Appeal Court for Moravia established in Brno. Towns deprived of the right of proclaiming capital sentences. 1753 Order providing for inhabitants' census issued. The first took place in 1754 in Bohemia, with the result amounting to 1.97 million inhabitants, 1.04 million in Moravia and Silesia. 1754 first Provincial Forest Regulations for Bohemia and Moravia issued. 1756 outbreak of the so-called Seven Years' War aimed at reacquiring Silesia. 1756 Austrian army defeated by Prussian troops of King Friedrich II. In May 1757 another defeat of Austrians in the battle at Štěrboholy. In June 1757 Friedrich II defeated, on his part at Kolín. War continued with intermittent luck, Maria Theresia's troops did not manage to dominate Silesia this time either. 1763 Peace of Hubertsburg (not far from Leipzig) put an end to Seven Years' War between Austria and Prussia. Maria Theresia gave up Silesia and Kladsko definitely. Prussia left Saxony. Friedrich II obliged himself to give his vote as Elector to Archduke Joseph, son of Maria Theresia. 1762 Czecho-Austrian Court Office replacing the Directorium

1752 Foundation of Credit Bank Brno.

1753 - 1775 Reconstruction of Prague castle according to the project of Nicola Pacassi in a simple classistic style with richly adorned rococco interiors. Both styles replacing Baroque are typical Theresian styles.

1757 Death of Jan Václav Antonín Stamic, Czech composer.

1767 - 1769 Ignác František Platzer, Czech sculptor created a group of statues called "Gigants' Struggle" (gate of Prague castle).

1770s Rise of a "Učená společnost" (Scientific Society).

Fortifications founded (Terezín, Josefov).

1771 - 1772 Starvation and plague in Czech territories. About a tenth of inhabitants died out. Mass spread of potatoes.

1771 Peasant tumults in Bohemia.

1772 First division of Poland.

1773 Jesuite Order cancelled by Pope Clement XIV.

1774 Compulsory school attendance from 6 to 12 years of age introduced.

1775 Great Peasant tumult.

1775 Forced Labour Patent.

Strahov Monastery in Prague

for Public and Cameral Matters (from 1749) established, 1763 Memorandum of Václav Antonín Kounic regarding Provincial Administration in Bohemia issued. On its basis, Provincial Government instead of Representation and Chamber, headed by Supreme Purgrave in Bohemia and by Provincial Captain in Moravia, established. 1764 Archduke Joseph, son of Franz Lotharingian and Maria Theresia, elected Emperor of Rome and Germany. 1765, the same assumed reign over Roman realm after his father's death and became, in the same year, co-regent of Maria Theresia in Habsburg lands.

1776 Torture cancelled in capital crimes proceedings.

1777 Diocese of Olomouc promoted to Archdiocese.

1777 Religious tumults in Valašsko (part of Moravia).

1778 - 1779 Bavarian Hereditary War (the so-called potato-war).

1780 - 1790
JOSEPH II,
son of Maria Theresia,
King of Bohemia
and Hungary,
Emperor of Rome

In the course of his reign of 10 years' duration, Joseph brought about many profound reforms. On October 13, 1781, he issued Patent on Tolerance permitting, beside Catholic also Augsburgian, Helvetian and Protestant confessions. Catholic church kept its privileged position as regards church and education administration. End of religious oppression. On November 1, 1781 Patent on Serfhood Cancellation issued for Bohemia, Moravia and Silesia. The same interdicted nobility to prevent subjects from marrying and leaving lords' estate. 1783 Administration of Moravia and rest of Silesia unified (integrated). In the same year, general seminars training pro-Josephine

Catholic church subordinated to the Crown Cancellation of monasteries.

1782 University of Olomouc transformed into Lyceum.

Germanization of schools.

Press liberty, promotion and support of agriculture, commerce, industries, foundation of charitable institutes.

1783 Foundation of Nostitz's Theatre (since 1779 Statutory Theatre).

1784 The four Prague towns, i.e. Old Town, New Town, Minor Side and Hradčany integrated in united administrative complex with common municipal authority.

Romantism

Castle Hluboká nad Vltavou

priests, established. In April 1783, judiciary reorganized in Czech lands. In October 1784 Provincial Statutory Courts cancelled and their competence taken over by Statutory governments. As a result authority of congresses was limited, therefore they assembled no longer. 1785 - 1789 Josephinian tax-levying order surveying all of the economically treatable soil, issued. 1786 First part of General Civil Codex issued followed by Criminal Codex. In the same year new criminal courts established. 1789 Income-tax and urbarial Patent issued replacing serfdom by pecuniary payments. Both the tax and urbarial burden was not to exceed 30 % of gross real estate yield. Joseph II was a non-ceremonial sovereign. Therefore, he did not let himself be coronated either in Bohemia or in Hungary. He liked travelling abroad and making himself acquainted with reality using his own eyes. He presented himself under the name Count of Falkenstein. His dream of constituting a powerful enlightened monarchy never came true. Died in Vienna in 1790.

1784 New Educational Order in Prague University accepted.

1784 Science Company, 1790 Royal Company of Sciences founded.

In December 1786, Wolfang Amadeus Mozart's opera Figaro's Wedding put on stage in Nostitz's Theatre Prague.

1789 - 1794 Out-break of Great French Revolution.

1753 - 1829 Josef Dobrovský, Czech historian and philologist.

1783 Steam-engine invented in England - Onset of industrial revolution.

1790 - 1792
LEOPOLD II,
brother of Joseph II,
King of Bohemia
and Hungary,
Emperor of Rome

Leopold II two years' reign was characterized by numerous recessions to antijosephinian opposition of statuses, though his attitude was an enlightened one. 1790 Josephinian Income-tax and urbarial Patent withdrawn and General Seminars

1790 Matěj Václav Kramerius founded the publishing house named Czech Expedition.

1791 First European Exposition of Industrial Produce held in Prague.

71

Classicism
Statuses' Theatre in Prague

cancelled, principal Josephinian reforms, i.e. Tolerance Patent and serfdom abolition remaining untouched. On September 6, 1791, Leopold was coronated King of Bohemia in Prague.

1792 Anti-France Allied Treaty between Austria and Prussia signed.

1792 - 1835
FRANZ I,
son of Leopold II,
King of Bohemia
and Hungary,
until 1806
Emperor of Rome,
since 1804
Emperor of Austria

Coronation of Franz II as King of Bohemia under the name of Franz I held in Prague. This sovereign strengthened absolutism and introduced police regime in Habsburg-governed countries. Franz II's reign abounded in wars against revolutionary France and Napoleon. 1792 France declared war on Austria. 1793 - 1797 First Coalition War against France ended by Peace of Campoformium in 1797. 1799 - 1801 out break of second war against France ended by Peace of Lunéville in 1801. 1804 Franz II assumed title of hereditary Emperor of Austria under the name Franz I. 1805 Third war against France. Austria and Russia defeated by Napoleon's troops at Slavkov (in Moravia). The war ended in the same year by Peace of Pressburg (Bratislava). Rise of Rhine Union results in extinction of the Saint Roman Realm of German Nation. 1810 marriage of Archduchess Mary Louise, daughter of Franz II, to Napoleon Bonaparte. 1811 State bankruptcy took place in Austria as a consequence of the Monarchy's total exhaustion by wars. 1811 Civil Code for non-Hungarian countries issued.

1792 Stool of Czech language and Literature of the Prague University established.

1793 Second division of Poland.

1795 Third division of Poland. Independent Polish State was put to an end.

1796 Jakub Jan Ryba - Czech Christmas Mass.

1797 First cotton spinning mill in Bohemia (Verneřice u Děčína).

1799 Academy of Creative Arts founded in Prague.

1801 First sugar-beet refinery in Bohemia and Czech countries (Hořovice).

1802 Abolition of all-life military service.

1802 - 1822 Castle Kačina at Kutná Hora - Empire style in Bohemia.

1803 - 1807 First steam engine in Czech coutries (Brno) designed by František Josef Gerstner.

1804 First wool spinning machine in Czech countries (Brno).

Empire
Church of Josefov

The latter introduces unitary citizenship and thrusts the way of all citizens' equality before Law. 1813 rise of coalition comprising Austria, Russia and Prussia which beat Napoleon's troops in the Battle of Nations at Leipzig. Supreme Commander of Allied forces, in which Slavs from Austria and Russian countries exceeded Germans, was the Czech Lord Marshal Knight of Schwarzenberg, the battle outlay was elaborated by Jan Josef Radecký, his staff's chief. 1814 Long-term war period between anti-Napoleon coalition and France concluded by Peace of Paris. 1814 - 1815 Congress of Vienna held. The same enables Austria to make numerous territorial gains. Following Napoleon's final defeat, (100 days' Empire) Second Peace of Paris signed in 1815. Russian troops staying in Czech countries strikingly raised Czech people's conscience of Slav impertinence. After Napoleonianic wars, Austria accepted Russian Tzar's project to conclude a treaty of Christian sovereigns against "rebellious forces" in Europe and thus provide for a "perpetual peace". 1815 rise of Saint Alliance of Allied powers, i.e. Austria, Russia and Prussia. Later on, further European countries join this Alliance. Repeated restoration of absolutism of Austrian monarchy, with Chancellor Clemens Wenzel Lothar Metternich as its main supporter. In those difficult days, great hopes

1804 First steam kettle in Bohemia (Stráž nad Nisou).

1805 Great Battle of Three Emperors at Slavkov, Moravia.

1806 South-German and West-German States make up the Napoleon-subjected Rhine Union.

1806 Technical College founded in Prague.

1813 Battle at Chlumec and Přestanov.

1814 Silesian Museum founded in Opava.
1817 Moravian Museum founded in Brno.
April 15, 1818 National Museum founded in Prague.

1815 Josef Božek demonstrated his steam carriage and 1817 his steam ship.

1817 Manuscript of Králův Dvůr.
1818 Manuscript of Zelená Hora.

1821 First rolling mill in Czech countries (Ondřejovice u Zlatých Hor).

1824 - 1832 Construction of horse-drawn railroad Českć Budějovice - Linz.
1825 - 1836 Construction of horse-drawn railroad Prague - Lány.

1825 Foundation of Czech Savings Bank.

1828 Iron works Vítkovice founded.

Neo-Gothics

New Provost's Residence in the third courtyard of Prague Castle

of Czech patriots aroused by Language Decree of 1816, widening rights of the Czech language in education (the same cancelled by Court provision of 1821).

1831 - 1832 Cholera in Czech countries.

1831 Fund of Bohemia established.

1834 First issue of the journal České květy (Czech blossoms) published.

1835 - 1848
FERDINAND V,
son of Franz I,
King of Bohemia
and Hungary,
Emperor of Austria

1835 Ferdinand V ascended to the throne. His countenance yielded him the name "Dobrotivý" (nice). Because of his weakness of mind, he was incapable of holding the sway. Actual power was in the hands of Triumvirate composed of Clemens Wenzel Lothar Metternich, Franz Anton Kolowrat and Archduke Louis. By the end of 1844 rise of a secret political club named Repeal (Prague) associating progressively thinking members of Prague's intellectuals. 1846 Court Decret on Serfdom Purchase issued. The same enabled the subjects to get rid of serfdom in offering purchase either in money or in kind. On March 11, 1848, the secret political club named Repeal initiated summoning of Prague's inhabitants in Saint Wenceslas's watering place in Prague's New Town to approve the proposal of a petition addressed to the Emperor asking constitution of Czech Crown as integral political unity, equality of Czechs and Germans in all fields of public life, general purchase and cancellation of serfdom, introduction of local government, press liberty, gathering liberty, religious freedom and the like.

December 21, 1834, the song "Kde domov můj" (Where's my home) by František Škroup with Josef Kajetán Tyl's libretto performed for the first time.

1835 - 1839 Josef Jungmann published in Prague his five-volume Czech-German Dictionary.

1836 Karel Hynek Mácha published his poem "Máj" (May).

1836 First coke blast furnace in all of Austrian monarchy started in Vítkovice.

1836 First mechanical flax spinning mill in Czech countries (Mladé Buky) started.

1773 - 1847
Josef Jungmann

1787 - 1869
Jan Evangelista Purkyně

1793 - 1852
Jan Kollár

1797 - 1876
František Palacký

1799 - 1852
František Ladislav Čelakovský

Neo-Romanesque
St. Cyrillus and Method's Basilica in Prague - Karlin

On March 12, 1848 first gathering of Saint Wenceslas's Committee in Old Town Hall of Prague. On March 14, 1848, Saint Wenceslas's Committee negotiated and approved of final version of petition to Emperor. Under pressure of Vienna rebellion took place. 13 - 15 March 1848 constitutionality promised. March 19, 1848 Prague deputation departed to Vienna to present petition containing requirements of the whole Czech national movement to the Emperor. His response was a vague one. Therefore, another petition was prepared and handed over to the Emperor on March 23, 1848. This time, it was responded by Cabinet letter of the Government dated April 8, 1848. The response acknowledged principle of equality of language intercourse in State administration and education, promises to complement Czech Provincial Assembly by representatives of industries, well-to-do peasantry and the like. The requirement regarding unification of Czech Crown's countries in an integral entity was, however, to be treated by the prospective allnational Assembly. On April 10, 1848 National Committee, as organ of the Czech constitutional movement, was established. April 11, 1848, František Palacký wrote an open letter known as Letter to Frankfurt, refusing, in the name of Czech nation, integration of Bohemia in the prospective German Unity, considering

1836 - 1847 Construction of Ferdinand's Northern railway Vienna - Nový Bohumín.

1840 First public Czech ball held in Prague.

1841 First Czech wheel steamer put on water in Prague - Karlín.

1842 New Regulations of the Unity for furthering Czech industries issued.

1842 Christian Doppler, Professor of Technical College Prague, formulated his (socalled Doppler's) principle regarding optical and acoustic phenomena.

1842 Town brewery (nowaday's Prazdroj) found in Plzeň (Pilsen).

1842 - 1845 Construction of Northern railway Olomouc - Prague.

1843 Slovak as literary language.

1845 First weaver school in Czech countries founded in Dolní Adršpach (not far from Trutnov).

1846 Civic Center named "Měšťanská beseda" as a representative town facility founded in Prague.

1848 First issue of the weekly "Týdeník", paper for science and entertainment issued in Brno (Brünn).

1848 First issue of Prague's evening paper published.

Neo-Rennaisance
National Theatre in Prague

Austrian monarchy to be the best guarantee of Czech nation's free development, provided the Austrian monarchy be changed in constitutional federation of independent nations. As counter-balance of the National Committee, adherents of the whole-German idea found in Prague Constitutional Corporation putting forward integration of Bohemia in unified Germany. On April 25, 1848 government of Vienna presented its octroied Constitution withdrawn, however, leading to revolutionary Vienna's resistance on May 16, 1848. In Czech countries culminated the so-called Frankfurt Struggle. Frankfurt Parliament elections fixed to be held on May 20, 1848, were boycotted by Czech inhabitants. In Spring 1848 resistance against serfdom and other feudal liabilities started spreading all over the Czech countryside. June 2 - 12, 1848 Slav Congress held in Prague. The same results in the Appeal of Slavs assembled at the Congress, to European nations to unite in refusing political and national oppresion. On June 12, 1848 (Whitsun Monday), students' tumults lacking any clear aims break out in Prague still in the course of Slav Congress. The rebellion of radically-minded youth was broken by the troops of commanding general Knight Windischgrätz. Thus, the results of Palacký's mild politics were ruined. On July 22, 1848 Czech

1848 Czech political corporation named "Lípa slovanská" (Slav lime-tree) founded.

1848 Historian František Palacký started publishing Czech translation of his all-life work "Dějiny národu českého v Čechách a v Moravě" (History of the Czech nation in Bohemia and Moravia; original written in German and entitled Geschichte von Böhmen). Since the third volume original written in Czech and translated to German.

1848 Failure of efforts to found a German realm.

1808 - 1856
Josef Kajetán Tyl

1810 - 1836
Karel Hynek Mácha

1811 - 1870
Karel Jaromír Erben

1818 - 1903
František Ladislav Rieger

1820 - 1862
Božena Němcová

1820 - 1871
Josef Mánes

1821 - 1856
Karel Havlíček Borovský

1824 - 1884
Bedřich Smetana

1834 - 1891
Jan Neruda

1841 - 1901
Julius Zeyer

Franz Joseph I

Constitutional Assembly was opened in Vienna. The only major deed of this assembly was the Act of September 7, 1848 abolishing serfdom. On October 6, 1848 a rebellion broke out in Vienna, and the Assembly was dislocated to Kroměříž (in Moravia), where it sat until March 7, 1849, when it was dispersed by the Army. Ferdinand V, the Emperor, took flight from revolutionary Vienna and put himself under protection of the Citadel of Olomouc.

1841 - 1904
Antonín Dvořák

1848 - 1916
FRANZ JOSEPH I,
nephew of Ferdinand V,
King of Hungary,
Emperor of Austria

In December 1848, Ferdinand V abdicated in Olomouc in fa-vour of his nephew Franz Joseph I. The inthronisation of the new Emperor was characterized by strengthening absolutism. Government dissolved Constitutional Imperial Assembly in Kroměříž and declared, on March 4, 1849 new octroied Constitution. Statuses were cancelled with a minor competence left to assemblies. Moravia and Silesia proclaimed Crown countries and, beside Czech kingdom, subjected directly to the Imperial Austrian Crown. On December 31, 1851, the octroied Constitution of 1849 cancelled by the so-called New Year's Eve Patents making the monarchy an absolute one. The most important representative of the regime became Alexander Bach, Minister of the Interior. Both the worsened foreign situation and financial short-comings following

1850 New Criminal Code issued.

1850 Telegraph for private correspondence in Czech countries used.

1850 First post-stamps of Habsburg monarchy issued.

1851 New Custom's Duty Tariff introduced in Austria. Protectionism moderated.

1853 - 1855 Krym War.

1858 Almanac "Máj" issued.

1859 Battles of Magenta and Solferino. Austria, in war against Sardinia, lost Lombardia.

1860 First issue of the journal "Čas" (time) published.

1861 Protestant Patent bestowing equal rights on Protestant and official Catholic confession issued.

Neo-Baroque
Stone Spa Teplice

Italian War lead to regime's breakdown. In August 1859 Alexander Bach was dismissed. 1860, Emperor Franz Joseph I issued the so-called October Diploma by which he gave up absolutism and accentuated importance of provincial assemblies. On February 1861 the so-called February Constitution proclaimed. This constitution showed a character completely different from that of October Diploma laying emphasis on monarchy's centralism. 1863 deputies of the Czech Assembly leave the Imperial Council. This passive opposition of the Czech toward Imperial Council lasted up to 1879. 1867 Austro-Hungarian Settlement took place. Consequently, monarchy split into two independent State formations joined by Union: "Předlitavsko" influenced by Vienna and "Zalitavsko", i.e. territory beyond Litava river - Hungary. On June 1867 the Settlement was solemnly confirmed (ratified) by coronation of Franz Joseph I as King of Hungary. The negotiations regarding the Settlement formally accomplished by December Constitution only, valid up until to the monarchy's breakdown. On August 22, 1868 Czech deputies of Provincial Assembly in Prague issued a political declaration against the monarchy's dualism. 1870 and 1871 Imperial rescripts issued displaying Franz Joseph I as interested

1862 Foundation of Slovak Fund in Turčiansky Svätý Martin.

1862 Sokol (falk) Association of Physical Culture founded.

1864 Austrian and Prussian troops in war against Denmark.

1865 František Palacký published his work Idea of the Austrian State.

1865 Regular steam navigation of Vltava-river started.

1866 Battle at Hradec Králové ended with Austria's defeat by Prussia.

1866 Czech and Austrian countries excluded from German Union.

1867 North-German Union founded.

1867 Pilgrimage of Czech politicians to Russia.

1868 Foundation stone for the National Theatre laid.

1868 Act on National Defense passed. General military duty introduced in Austria (for a three year period).

1868 Almanac "Ruch" (traffic) issued.

1869 Czech Polytechnical College split into Czech and German parts. The Czech part established as Czech Technical University.

1869 Rise of Škoda Enterprises in Plzeň (Pilsen).

Habsburg monarchy territory in 1914

1526 ~ 1918

PRZEMYŚL

BUKOVINA

KRAKÓW

KOŠICE

TRANSYLVANIA

NITRA

BUDAPEST

BRATISLAVA

HUNGARY

OPAVA

MORAVIA

BRNO

BOHEMIA

PRAGUE

PASSAU

Danube

LINZ

VIENNA

AUSTRIA

SALZBURG

Sava

OSIJEK

SERBIA

SARAJEVO

BOSNIA

HERZEGOVINA

MOSTAR

NOVI PAZAR

ZAGREB

CROATIA

DALMATIA

TRST

TIROL

TRIDENT

in the coronation as King of Bohemia. Czech Provincial Assembly accepted the so-called Fundamental Articles deliniating the political status of Bohemia in the framework of monarchy. Negative standpoint of Germans and Hungarians within the monarchy ruins, however, the efforts to bring about Czecho-Austrian Settlement. Thus, the coronation of Franz Joseph I as King of Bohemia never came true. During the reign of Franz Joseph I, Czech language spread, to a greater extent, on both primary and secondary education. According to language regulations of Karl von Stremayr (1880) and Count Kazimír Badeni (1897), Czech started being used even as an official language. 1890 negotiations as regards the so-called Punctation Articles based on efforts to achieve Czecho-German settlement in the monarchy's framework were started. Struggles for language right in Bohemia, roused by punctations (i.e. Czecho-German settlement) then continue till extinction of Austro-Hungarian monarchy. 1905 Emperor Franz Joseph I confirmed the so-called Moravian Treaty. Thus, in Moravia at least, Czecho-Austrian Settlement succeeded. Moravian Assembly was given Czech majority with German minority being secured as well. On January 26, 1907 General right of election for males over 24 years

1869 Act on General Compulsory School Attendance passed. Attendance prolonged to eight years basically.

1872 "První brněnská strojírna" (First Brünn Machine Works) founded.

1871 Rise of the German Imperium.

1873 Act on Direct Elections to Imperial Council, the so-called April Constitution passed.

1874 Town-walls demolition started in Prague.

1874 National Liberal Party (Young Czechs) founded by separation from National Party (Old Czechs).

1876 Death of Ferdinand I, last coronated King of Bohemia Following his abdication in 1848 he lived in Prague Castle enjoying great popularity among Prague's inhabitants.

1876 One month after the conclusion of his all-life work "History of the Czech Nation in Bohemia and Moravia" František Palacký died.

1878 Occupation of Bosnia and Hercegovina by Habsburg monarchy.

1846 - 1908
Svatopluk Čech

1850 - 1937
Tomáš Garrigue Masaryk

1850 - 1900
Zdeněk Fibich

Secession
Principal Railroad Station Prague

of age introduced in Předlitavsko. In May 1907 election of Imperial Council held. Out of Czech political parties, the Agricultural Party acquired 28 seats, Social-Democrats 24 seats, Young Czechs 18 seats, Clericals 17 seats, National Socials 9 seats, Old Czechs 7 seats, Progress Party 2 all-seats and Independent Candidates 2 seats respectively. Out of the national groups sitting in the House of Deputies of the Imperial Assembly 232 were Germans, 108 Czechs, 79 Polish, 32 Ukrainians, 24 Slovenians, 19 Italians, 13 Serbo-Croatians, 7 Rumanians and 4 Jews respectively. In the period between February and March 1908 elections of Czech Provincial Assembly were held. The Assembly was opened in September 1908. Its legislative activities were, however, disturbed by feuds between Czech and German deputies. 1913 Czech Assembly was dissolved and replaced by Administrative Commision subordinated to the Sovereign directly. Until the outbreak of the World War, the Assembly never reassumed their activities. On June 28, 1914 assassination of Ferdinand d'Este, successor to the throne, and his spouse Sofia committed by a group of Serb students in Sarajevo. On July 7, 1914, Ministerial Council decided to present Serbia wide-spread requirements supposed to be denied and military intervention made inevitable. On July 28,

1882 Division of Carlo-Ferdinand University.

1883 Opening of the National Theatre.

1886 Manuscript discrepancy proved falsehood of Králův Dvůr and Zelená Hora manuscripts.

1888 Otto's Encyclopedia starts appearing.

1889 Poldina huť (Poldi's Iron Works) founded in Kladno.

1890 Czech Academy of Arts and Sciences founded.

1891 Anniversary Provincial Exposition in Prague.

1892 Crown currency introduced.

1895 Czecho-Slav folklore Exhibition in Prague.

1896 First power-driven tram in Prague.

1897 First Combustion engine-driven car marque President made in Czech countries (Kopřivnice).

1899 Czech Olympic Committee founded.

1901 Czech Philharmonic Orchestra founded.

1908 Annexion of Bosnia and Hercegowina by Habsburg monarchy.

Czech Cubism

Cubistic family house in Prague - Vyšehrad

1914 Austro-Hungary declared war on Serbia. In December 1914, T. G. Masaryk went abroad and started, in July 1915 in Geneva, a foreign anti-Austrian campaign aimed at constituting independent Czechoslovakia. Later on, he founded, together with Edvard Beneš, a foreign Committee associating all Czech organizations abroad. In February 1916, the Czech Foreign Committee changed to Czechoslovak National Council in Paris. On November 1916, death of Emperor Franz Joseph I.

On August 1, 1914 Czech Military group "Nazdar" founded.

On August 1914, Committee of Czech Settlers and Volunteers founded in Prague.

September 1914 battle at Marne.

1915 Czech Community "Sokol" dissolved.

1916 - 1918
KARL I,
grand-nephew
of Franz Joseph I,
King of Hungary,
Emperor of Austria

Gradual strengthening of Czech and Slovak nations' Liberation movement headed by Tomáš Garrigue Masaryk, Edvard Beneš and Milan Rastislav Štefánik in the course of World War I. Out of Czech and Slovak deserters, prisoners-of-war and foreign compatriots were formed military legions fighting at the side of Russian, French and Italian troops against Central Powers, i.e. Germany and Austro-Hungary. At the head of the inland independence struggle were Karel Kramář, Alois Rašín and Přemysl Šámal. Representatives of the home independence struggle unite in the secret organization called Maffia striving to integrate with foreign anti-Austrian resistance. At Maffia's head stood first E. Beneš and, after his going abroad, P. Šámal. 1916 K. Kramář

1851 - 1930
Alois Jirásek

1852 - 1913
Mikoláš Aleš

1853 - 1912
Jaroslav Vrchlický

1854 - 1928
Leoš Janáček

Modernism

Kotěra's villa in Prague - Vinohrady

and A. Rašín sentenced to death by Austrian Courts, however, amnestied in 1917. On August 1917, French government concluded a treaty with Czechoslovak National Council as regards Czechoslovak Army. On the basis of this treaty, National Council became, on December 16, 1917 Supreme political authority of Czechoslovak troops in France. On January 6, 1918, the so-called Epophary Declaration accepted in Prague, at a gathering of Czech imperial and provincial deputies. The Declaration insisted on self-determination of nations and integration of Czech countries with Slovakia. On May 30, 1918 representatives of Czech and Slovak organizations in the United States, and T. G. Masaryk signed the Pittsburg Convention approving of the integration of Czech and Slovaks in one independent State union. On June 29, 1918, French government proclaimed the right of Czechoslovak nation to become independent and acknowledged Czechoslovak National Council publicly as a supreme organ providing for all national interests, and first basis of the next Czechoslovak government. On July 13, 1918 reorganization of Czechoslovak National Committee as supreme home national and political organ. On August 9, 1918 government of Great Britain acknowledged Czechoslovak National Council as representative of Czechoslovak

On January 17, 1917 Czechoslovak Volunteers Corps founded in Italy.

On April 1917, United States declares war on Germany.

On May 17, 1917 Address of Czech writers to deputies in Imperial Council.

July 2, 1917 Battle at Zborov. A Czechoslovak brigade beat troops of Central powers. This was the first independent action of the Czechoslovak Army in Russia.

October 9, 1917 Czechoslovak Army Corps founded in Russia.

November 7, 1917 October revolution in Russia.

March 3, 1918 Armistice between Central Powers and Soviet Russia signed in Brestlitevsk.

BANKA LEGIY

Decorativism - arch style
Legiobank in Prague - New Town

national interests and predecessor of future Czechoslovak government. So did, on September 3, 1918, the government of the United States. On September 26, 1918 the provisional Czechoslovak government with T. G. Masaryk, as its President, Head of Ministerial Council and Secretary of Finances, E. Beneš, as Foreign Minister and Milan Rastislav Štefánik as Minister of Defense established. The Provisory Czech government was then acknowledged by France, Great Britain, Serbia, Italy etc. On October 16, 1918, Emperor Karl I issued the Manifest proclaiming federalization of Austria presuming establishment of four states, i.e. Germano-Austrian, Czech, Yugoslav and Ukrainian. The Emperor did not dare to provide, in this way, self-determination of nations in Hungary. The effort of Emperor Karl I to federalize Austria was a failure, for political aims of individual nations in Austria prove to be beyond his possibilities. On October 18, 1918 Masaryk published in Washington, in the name of the Czechoslovak government, Declaration of Czechoslovak Independence comprising main constitutional principles outlined in the sense of republican ideas of Czechoslovak State. This declaration was issued as reaction of Czechoslovak Provisory government to peace offers of Central Powers, i.e. Austria, Hungary and Germany.

July - August, 1918 Second battle on Marne.

1860 - 1937
Karel Kramář

1867 - 1923
Alois Rašín

1867 - 1937
František Xaver Šalda

1868 - 1929
Otokar Březina

95

Tomáš Garrigue Masaryk

1918 - 1937
Dr. TOMÁŠ
GARRIGUE MASARYK,
President of Czechoslovak
Republic

On October 28, 1918 National Committee passed in Prague Act of Establishment of Independent Czechoslovak State. On October 30, 1918 Slovak National Council accepted, in Turčiansky Sv. Martin, Declaration of the Slovak nation, as decision to integrate Slovaks as a part of the common State of Czechs and Slovaks. On November 13, 1918, National Committee proclaimed Provisional Constitution. On November 14, 1918 first session of National Assembly where democratic form of the Czechoslovak State was proclaimed, took place. T. G. Masaryk was elected President, and Karel Kramář Prime Minister of the newly established government. Czechoslovak Republic (ČSR) was composed of Czech historical countries Bohemia, Moravia, Czech Silesia and, further on, of Slovakia and Carpatho-Russia. Apart from that, minor territories of Vitorazy, Valtice and Hlučín were annexed to ČSR. The frontiers of the new Republic were set by Peace Treaty of Versailles concluded with Germany on June 28, 1919, Peace of Saint Germain concluded with Austria on September 10, 1919 Treaty of Trianon concluded with Hungary on June 14, 1920, further on by special treaties concluded with Romania on August 10, 1920 and Poland on February 7, 1921, the frontiers of Těšín, Orava and Spiš areas being fixed

1873 - 1933
Antonín Švehla

1877 - 1931
Viktor Dyk

1890 - 1938
Karel Čapek

February 1919 Rise of Czechoslovak currency; bills issued by Austro-Hungarian bank stamped.

April 1919 Bill on Agricultural Reform referring to confiscation of real estates over 150 hectares of arable soil or over 250 hectares of soil altogether.

May 4, 1919 Brno and Bratislava Universities founded.

1919 War between Hungary and Czechoslovakia.

1919 Rise of German political parties DNP and DNSAP.

January 16, 1920 Opening session of United Nations. Czechoslovakia was one of its founding members.

February 19, 1920 Czech University of Prague Charles's University reestablished.

97

Prague · Old Town Square

by Allied Council of Ambassadors. As to national groups involved, ČSR proved to be a heterogenous State formation. Czechs and Slovaks considered to be two branches of one and the same nation, made up about 65% of all inhabitants. According to 1921 census, 13 613 172 inhabitants lived on the territory of the Republic, out of whom 6 850 000 Czechs (51%), 1 910 000 Slovaks (14.5%), 3 123 000 Germans (23.4%), 745 000 Hungarians (5.5%), 461 000 Carpatho-Russians, Ukrainians and Russins, 180 000 Jews, 75 000 Poles as well as minor groups of other nationalities. Czech and Slovak official languages of the Republic. ČSR inherited 60-70% of Austro-Hungarian industries. There were, however, discrepancies as to dislocation of the latter. Whereas Czech countries could be looked upon as those with well-developed industry, Slovakia and Carpatho-Russia remained backward agricultural ones. On July 8, 1919 Czechoslovak government headed by Vlastimil Tusar was appointed. February 29, 1920 National Assembly approved of a Constitution formally proclaiming Czechoslovakia as democratic Republic with an eligible President at its head. On May 27, 1920 T. G. Masaryk elected President of the Republic for the second time. On September 15, 1920 State Servants' government of Jan Černý appointed. 1921

March 1920 The Slovak National Theatre started its artistical activities.

March 1920 Defence Act providing for military duty of males of 20 - 50 years of age and military service of 18 month duration.

1919 - 1920 Czechoslovak legions leave Russia on Siberian railroads to Vladivostok and, further on, by ship, to Europe.

Czechoslovak legions played an important part in military activities of the Alliance. All in all 55 000 Czechoslovak legionaires fought in Russia, 20 000 in Italy and 9 000 in France.

October 1920 Artistic Company "Devětsil" founded.

1921 Czechoslovak Communist Party founded.

Constructivism and Functionalism

Former General Pension Institute in Prague

Allied treaties between Czechoslovakia, Romania and the Kingdom of Serbians, Croatians and Slovenians (SHS) signed. This military Union was called the Minor Alliance. On September 26, 1921 Czechoslovak government headed by Edvard Beneš was appointed. On October 23, 1921 Czechoslovak Republic and the Kingdom of Serbians, Croatians and Slovenians (SHS) declared partial mobilization against repeated effort of Karl I, ancient Emperor to assume reign over Hungary. Karl of Habsburg died on April 1, 1922, in the course of his imprisonment in Madeira. On October 7, 1922 Czechoslovak government, headed by Antonín Švehla, appointed. 1924 Allied treaty between Czechoslovakia and France signed. 1923 communal elections took place. On July 6, 1925 national celebrations held at the occasion of Jan Hus's name-day lead to discrepancies between Czechoslovakia and the Vatican. Pope's nuncio Marmaggi left Prague. The conflict results in signing the so-called Modus vivendi on December 17, 1927. On March 18, 1926 Civil Servants' government of Jan Černý appointed to be replaced, in the same year (October 12) by government headed by A. Švehla. On May 27, 1927 T. G. Masaryk elected President of the Republic for the third time. On December 2, 1928 elections to

1926 National Bank of Czechoslovakia starts its activities.

1929 - 1934 World economical crisis.

Edvard Beneš

the Provincial Boards of Representatives took place. On February 1, 1929 government headed by František Udržal appointed. On October 27, 1929 elections to National Assembly. On October 29, 1932 government headed by Jan Malypetr appointed. On February 16, 1933 organizational Treaty of Entente intended to coordinate foreign politics of Czechoslovak republic, signed. This was, as a matter of fact, a permanent Council of Entente to coordinate foreign politics of Czechoslovakia, Yugoslavia and Romania. On May 24, 1934 T. G. Masaryk elected President of the Republic for the fourth time. On June 9, 1934 Czechoslovak Republic started diplomatic relations with Soviet Union. On May 16, 1935 Allied treaty between Czechoslovakia and Soviet Union, depending on support of France, signed. On November 5, 1935 government headed by Milan Hodža appointed. On December 14, 1935 T. G. Masaryk gave up his presidency.

1933 Adolf Hitler became Reich Chancellor.

October 2, 1933 Heinlein's Sudetendeutsche Heimatsfront (SHF) founded.

1933 Prohibition of German political parties DNP and DNSAP activities.

1934 Secretary of Education issued decret ordering German university to hand insignia universitatis out to Charles's University.

1935 - 1938
Dr. EDVARD BENEŠ,
President
of the Czechoslovak
Republic
(1940 - 1945 in exile)

On December 18, 1935 Edvard Beneš elected new President. On April 24, 1938 Konrad Henlein proclaimed in Karlovy Vary at the Congress of SdP, his Eight-Point Programme requiring Sudeten autonomy. In August 1938, British government sent off to Czechoslovakia Lord Runciman as independent examiner and mediator to take part in

1936 - 1939 Civil war in Spain.

September 14, 1937 First President of Czechoslovak Republic T. G. Masaryk died.

CZECHOSLOVAK REPUBLIC

1918-1938

BOHEMIA

PLZEŇ

PRAGUE

OLOMOUC

BRNO

MORAVIA

SLOVAKIA

KOŠICE

NITRA

BRATISLAVA

UZHGOROD

CARPATHO RUSSIA

negotiations of Czechoslovak government with Sudeten Party. Out of Runciman's report addressed to British government could be deduced that there was no possibility whatsoever of further co-existence of the Czechs and the Germans in a common State. Great Britain and France inclined to Germany and started forcing Czechoslovak government representation to make concessions to both Henlein and Hitler. On September 1938 President E. Beneš appointed a new Czechoslovak government headed by Jan Syrový, General of Army. This gave way to general hopes the Republic is ready to defend its independence. On September 23, 1939 Czechoslovak Republic proclaimed mobilization. On September 29, 1939 representatives of Germany (Hitler), Italy (Mussolini), Great Britain (Chamberlain) and France (Daladier) signed in Munich Convention on cession of boundary Czechoslovak territories to Germany. On September 30, 1938 Czechoslovak President E. Beneš and government, abandoned by their allies, were forced to accept, in spite of broad public resistance, the dictation of Munich. In following weeks, Czech boundary regions were annexed to Germany, Těšín area to Poland, and southern parts of Slovakia and Carpatho-Russia to Hungary. On October 5, 1938, President E. Beneš abdicated and flew to England. Czechoslovakia's

March 1938 Annexion of Austria. Austrian Republic eredicated by Germany.

1938 Assault on Czechoslovak Republic named Fall Grün (Case Green) prepared.

May 1938 Manifest reading "We'll keep our Loyalty" issued. The same signed by over 1 million inhabitants of the Czechoslovak Republic until the end of September.

July 1938 Tenth nation-wide "Sokol" gathering held in Prague.

division was concluded by Arbitration of Vienna (November 2, 1938). On November 19, 1938, National Assembly passed in Prague Act of Slovak and Carpatho-Russian autonomies. The official designation of the State was then Czecho-Slovakia.

1938 - 1945
Dr. EMIL HÁCHA,
President
of Czecho-Slovakia,
eventually the so-called
State President

On November 30, 1938 Dr. Emil Hácha elected Czechoslovak President. On March 15, 1939 after elapse of half-a-year of the so-called Second Republic, ČSR was definitely occupied by German troops and the so-called Protectorate Bohemia and Moravia established. On the eve of March 14, 1939, Slovak Republic was proclaimed in Bratislava as formally independent formation but, as a matter of fact, standing under the influence of Germany. Dr. Josef Tiso became President, clerofascist regime established. Rest of Carpatho-Russia annexed to Hungary. After breakdown of the Republic both the domestic and foreign resistances formed. Gradually Czechoslovak foreign military units, first rose in Poland, France and Great Britain, later on in Soviet Union. On July 9, 1940 a State formation of the Czechoslovak Republic in exile headed by Dr. E. Beneš was established and acknowledged by Great Powers in July 1941. On August 5, 1942 British government withdrew its signature of Munich Convention. On September 29, 1942 French

September 1, 1939 German troops assault Poland.

November 15, 1939 Funeral of the student Jan Opletal took place.
November 17, 1939 Closure of all Czech Universities and Technical Colleges. 9 students executed, 1200 students brought to concentration camps.

June 22, 1940 Capitulation of France. Prior to that occupation of a substantial part of North and South Europe.

Summer 1940 Air battle over Great Britain.

June 22, 1941 Germany attacks Soviet Union.

January 1941 - November 1942 struggles at Tobruk. Significant participation of a Czechoslovak military troop.

December 2, 1941 Japanese Air Force attacks American Navy at Pearl Harbor, Hawaii. The attack ruined part of American Pacific Fleet and made USA enter World War II.

May 27, 1942 Assault on R. Heydrich.

National Committee headed by General de Gaulle proclaimed Munich Convention as void since the very beginning. So did, later on (September 26, 1944), the Italian government. Apart from London Centre, also Moscow Communist Centre, headed by Klement Gottwald, played quite a significant role within foreign resistance. Domestic resistance was represented by a wide spectrum of Antinazi forces. The resistance was suppressed by Nazi power in an utmost hard way. Gradually, a political shift to the left became manifest. On December 12, 1943 Dr. E. Beneš signed in Moscow a new allied Czechoslovak Soviet treaty. By the end of the war, Czechoslovak exile representation became increasingly influenced by Soviet political power. The liberation struggle of Czechs and Slovaks culminated by Slovak National Rebellion of August 29 - October 27, 1944 and that of Prague (May 5 - 9, 1945) ended by Red Army arrival in Prague. According to the Convention of Great Powers most was liberated by troops of Soviet Army. Western and Southern parts of Bohemia were liberated by American troops.

1945 - 1948
Dr. EDVARD BENEŠ,
President
of the Czechoslovak
Republic

On May 16, 1945 President E. Beneš came back to Prague. Right after the liberation, the independent Czechoslovak Republic was restored. According to treaty of June 19, 1945 Carpatho-Russia annexed to

June 10, 1942 Extermination of Lidice.

June 24, 1942 Extermination of the settlement Ležáky.

August 1942 - February 1943 Battle at Stalingrad. Red Army's victory and Pacific battlefield reversal were breaking points of World War II.

January 30, 1943 First Czechoslovak Independent Battalion left for front at Buzuluk.

March 8, 1943 Battle at Sokolovo.

June 6, 1944 Allied forces disembarkation at Normandy.

September 8, 1944 Start of the Carpatho-Russian operation.

October 6, 1944 Members of the First Czechoslovak Army Corps in Soviet Union, fighting in 38th division of the First Ukrainian Front, step on the soil of their motherland in Dukla pass region.

April 21, 1945 Units of the Third American army headed by General G. Patton enter Czechoslovak territory taking Aš. After that, American army marched across Bohemia and, on May 6, arrived in Plzeň (Pilsen) taking the line Plzeň - Karlovy Vary.

April 5, 1945 Czechoslovak government approved of the so-called Košice governmental programme.

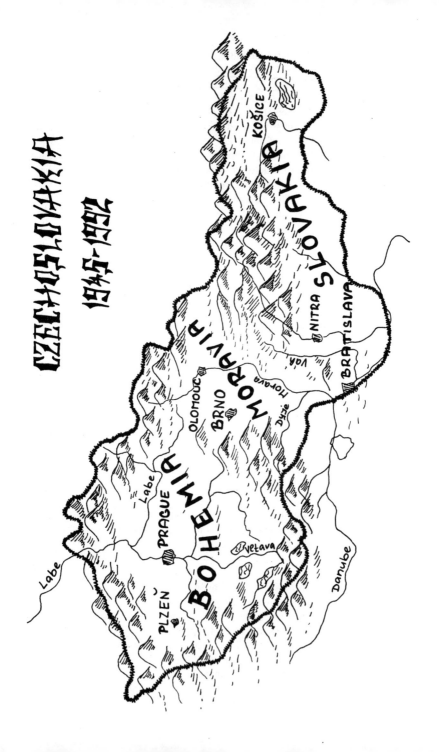

CZECHOSLOVAKIA
1945-1992

KOŠICE

SLOVAKIA

NITRA

BRATISLAVA

Váh

MORAVIA

OLOMOUC

BRNO

Morava

Dyje

Labe

PRAGUE

Labe

BOHEMIA

Vltava

PLZEŇ

Danube

Soviet Union. On October 24, 1945 President E. Beneš signed Nationalization Decrets. On November 1, 1945 new Czechoslovak crown (as currency unit) introduced. Czechoslovak Republic started edificating the system of the so-called People's Democracy. On May 26, 1945 Elections to Constitutional Assembly held, banning, according to the governmental programme of Košice, all political parties which were not members of the National Front. In May elections 1946, Communists, who were given more than 40% votes in Czech countries, were victorious. On June 19, 1946, Dr. E. Beneš reelected President. On July 2, 1946, new Czechoslovak government, with K. Gottwald at its head, appointed. On February 25, 1948 in an atmosphere created by demonstrations of Communist adherents and presumptive threat of civil war, President Dr. E. Beneš accepted demission of democratic Ministers, as well as Communist requirement to appoint new government composed mostly of Communists and their supporters. Thus, the Communist Party of Czechoslovakia took over the power in ČSR. Soon after February 1948, all features of a parliamentary democratic system were removed and replaced by a totalitarian dictatorship of the Communist Party of Czechoslovakia. On May 9, a new constitution, legalizing the

May 12, 1945 Following fights at Milín (in Bohemia) World War II put to an end in Europe.

June 26, 1945 United Nations Charter signed in San Francisco. Czechoslovak Republic becoming its founding member.

July 17 - August 2, 1945 Conference under participation of the United States, Soviet Union and Great Britain held at Postdam.

August 6, 1945 American atomic bomb dropped on Hiroshima. August 9, 1945 second atomic bomb dropped on Nagasaki.

September 2, 1945 Japan's capitulation put an end to World War II.

1945 - 1946 Germans transferred out of Czechoslovakia.

November 1, 1946 Germans' transfer achieved officially. Altogether about 2 256 000 persons were transferred to Germany, the remnants of German inhabitants making out about 1.8%.

June 3, 1947 UNRRA's activities finished.

In July 1947 The so-called Marshall's Plan of America's Economic Aid to European countries discussed, Albania, Bulgaria, Czechoslovakia, Finland, Yugoslavia, Hun-gary, Poland and Romania forced by Soviet Union not to take part in the Plan.

Postwar Urbanism
Tower tenement houses
dating from the period 1948 - 1950 in Zlín

new reality, accepted. On June 7, 1948 President E. Beneš resigned and, 3 months later, on September 3, 1948 died.

March 13, 1948 State funeral of Jan Masaryk, Foreign Minister, who died on March 10, 1948 under obscure circumstances.

1948 - 1953
KLEMENT GOTTWALD,
President
of the Czechoslovak
Republic

On June 14, 1948 Klement Gottwald elected new President. Gradually, a total nationalization of industry and commerce carried out and a violent collectivization of agriculture set on. Press speech and confession liberties of the inhabitants made thoroughly impossible or repressed. Arts and culture subjected to ideological monopoly of the Communist Party of Czechoslovakia. In January, 1949 Provincial governmental system was cancelled and replaced by District governmental system. Gradually, market economy replaced by centralized planning system. On January 5 - 8, 1949 Council of Mutual Economic Assistance established in Moscow with Bulgaria, Czechoslovakia, Hungary, Romania, Poland and Soviet Union as member-countries. Later, Albania, German Democratic Republic and Mongolia joined. In the sphere of foreign politics, Czechoslovakia became a solid integral part of the Soviet power block. The first half of fifties was unpropitiously famous by political lawsuits whose victims were not only adversaries of the Communist regime, such as Milada Horáková and the like, but Communists, such as Rudolf Slánský and others.

Post-February emigration wave.

April 4, 1949 North-Atlantic Treaty Organization (NATO) signed in Washington.

November 17, 1952 Czechoslovak Academy of Sciences founded.

111

Workers
Motive of a hundred crowns' banknote issued in 1961

the lawsuits themselves and State administration took a direct part Soviet councellours. On March 14, 1953 President K. Gottwald died.

1953 - 1957
ANTONÍN ZÁPOTOCKÝ,
President
of the Czechoslovak
Republic

Antonín Zápotocký elected new President. On June 1, 1953 currency reform took place. Cashes and deposits exchanged in the ratio 1:5 to 1:50. On May 14, 1953 rise of the military Union Warsaw Treaty with Czechoslovakia, Albania, Bulgaria, Hungary, German Democratic Republic, Poland, Romania and Soviet Union as founding member-states. On November 13, 1957 A. Zápotocký died.

February 25, 1954 Czechoslovak Television started broadcasting.

1955 First all-national Spartakiade held in Prague.

1956 20th Congress of the Communist Party of Soviet Union held. There, though unconsequently, the so-called personality worship criticized for the first time.

1956 Extinction of the anti-Communist Rebellion in Hungary. Also in Poland tumults of the inhabitants against Communist regime took place.

1957 - 1968
ANTONÍN NOVOTNÝ,
President
of the Czechoslovak
Republic
(since 1960 of Czechoslovak
Socialist Republic)

Antonín Novotný elected President of the Republic on November 19, 1957. On July 11, 1960 National Assembly approved the new Constitution emphasizing the leading role of the Communist Party of Czechoslovakia in society. New official name of the State-Czechoslovak Socialist Republic (ČSSR) and a new State emblem were accepted. 1960 further reform of State administration with new "great" regional governments established. In the sixties a partial moderation, particularly in ideology and culture, took place. Simultaneously, striking economic problems arose, the position of Slovakia, within the hitherto

1960 Second all-national Spartakiade took place in Prague.

1965 Third all-national Spartakiade in Prague.

1967 Strahov tumults and Fourth Congress of Czechoslovak Writers.

Alexander Dubček

unitarian State, became an increasingly crucial issue. A vast effort to bring about economic reform became visible. At January session of the Central Committee of the Communist Party of Czechoslovakia held in 1968, Alexander Dubček was elected it's First Secretary. On March 22, 1968 Antonín Novotný gave up his presidency.

1968 - 1975
LUDVÍK SVOBODA,
President of the
Czechoslovak Socialist
Republic

On March 30, 1968 Ludvík Svoboda elected President. On April 8, 1968 new government headed by Oldřich Černík appointed by the President. In April 1968 Josef Smrkovský became new head of National Assembly. Both the new government and the old-new Parliament started preparing federal state organization. At its April session, Central Committee accepted Action Programme of the Communist Party of Czechoslovakia and, by the end of May, at its plenary session, it agreed with introduction of a market model of national economy as projected by Ota Šik. Moderated conditions in cultural and political life gave rise to new organizations, such as the Club of Engaged Non-Party-Members, K 231, which were becoming a basis of pluralist democracy. Censorship was paralyzed. Reform Communists strove for Communism with a human face. On June 27, 1968 in some of the newspapers appeared the "2000 Words

First steps taken towards restoration of Social-Democratic Party.

Socialist Realism
Ostrava - Poruba

Declaration" suggesting that the reform process was to carry on without or, if necessary, against the interests of the Communist party of Czechoslovakia. The reviving process of Czechoslovak society called "Prague's Spring" by both the domestic and foreign journalists, was violently brought to an end by armed intervention of Warsaw Treaty Member-States on August 21, 1968. ČSSR was assaulted by 750 000 foreign soldiers armed with 6 000 tanks and a great amount of military technology. On August 23, 1968 Czechoslovak-Soviet negotiations took place. Czechoslovak delegation agreed with unlimited stay of Soviet military forces upon Czechoslovak territory. On set of the so-called normalization period. On October 27, 1968 Czechoslovak Federation Act passed by National Assembly. On April 1969 Gustáv Husák put at the head of the Central Committee of the Communist Party of Czechoslovakia. Wave of repressions against the inhabitants was started. The purification process afflicting all of the society lasted up to 1971.

August 22, 1968 Extraordinary Congress of the Communist party of Czechoslovakia held in Prague - Vysočany demands withdrawal of Soviet troops from Czechoslovak territory.

Onset of post-August emigration wave amounting to about 700 - 800 thousand persons.

January 16, 1969 The student Jan Palach committed suicide by self-burning.

1975 - 1989
GUSTÁV HUSÁK,
President of the
Czechoslovak Socialist
Republic

On May 1975 Gustáv Husák elected President of ČSSR. Innovation of an overall totalitarian system. Compulsory bureaucratic methods were applied not only in national economy control but also in

July 30 - August 1, 1975 Helsinki Conference on European Security and Cooperation held. Czechoslovakia signed its Final Act.

Václav Havel

culture, education and science. In the field of foreign politics, the Czechoslovak Party and State representation became one of the most consequential allies of Brezhnev's dictatorship in USSR. 1985, due to M. S. Gorbatschov's reform movement taking place in Soviet Union, some moderate reformatory efforts became apparent in ČSSR as well. The Communist Party of Czechoslovakia kept, however, its firm power monopoly. In November 1989 the long-term inner political tension led to an overwhelming opposition of citizens against the totalitarian power. The upheaval was caused by brutal intervention of Public State Security and Intelligence Service against students' demonstration held in National Avenue Prague on November 17, 1989. The Communist State representation, deprived of its foreign support capitulated handing its power to the Opposition. On December 1989, G. Husák abdicated, and the leading role of the Communist Party was cancelled. The November Revolution was called, because of its non-violent course, a "delicate" or "velvet" revolution.

January 1977 Charter 77 published.

January 1988 Antigovernment demonstrations, the so-called "Palach's Week" took place in Prague.

1989 - 1992
VÁCLAV HAVEL,
President
of the Czech and Slovak
Federal Republic

In December 1989 Václav Havel, representative of the hitherto dissent, elected Pre-sident. The official name of the State was changed to Czech and Slovak Federal Republic, so were simultaneously, also some of

State symbols. Parliamentary democracy restored in Czechoslovakia, gradually, a wide spectrum of political parties, civic organizations, administrative, economical and social institutions associated with the traditions of the ancient democratic Czechoslovak Republic were founded or rennovated. Quite a vast economical reform aimed at a full restoration of market economy, as well as State administration reform were started. On June 1990, free parliamentary elections won by Civic Forum (in the Czech Republic) and Public against Violence (in Slovakia) took place. Within the chaotic transient period and in a complex economic situation, problems, remaining unsolved for years, manifested. A particularly crucial problem became the issue of further coexistence of Czech and Slovak nations, and that of a new political image of the new Constitution. In June 1992 parliamentary elections took place, whose winners were the right-oriented Civic Democratic Party (ODS) headed by Václav Klaus in Czech countries and the left-oriented Movement for Democratic Slovakia (HZDS) headed by Vladimír Mečiar in Slovakia. The following discussion of both political parties showed that HZDS was ready to acquire independence for Slovakia. On July 17, 1992 at the meeting of the newly elected Slovak

January 9, 1991 Federal Assembly accepted Charter of Fundamental Human Rights and Liberties.

December 16, 1991 Convention on joining of ČSFR European Community signed.

February 29, 1992 Registration of the first wave coupon privatization concluded (Start November 1, 1991). In both republics 8 565 642 citizens registered.

November 3, 1992 Movement Charter 77 ended its activities.

November 7, 1992 Death of Alexander Dubček, Prague's Spring 1968 representative.

120

National Council, Declaration on Independence of Slovak Republic was accepted. On July 20, 1992 Václav Havel gave up his presidency of Czech and Slovak Federal Republic.

1992
non-presidential period

On September 1, 1992 Slovak National Council passed the Constitution of the Slovak Republic. On October 29, 1992 Prime Ministers of both the Czech and Slovak government, V. Klaus and Vl. Mečiar, signed 16 conventions on future cooperation between the Czech and Slovak Republics. The convention on Custom's Duty Union presuming introduction of unitary custom territory, as well as free merchandise and services motion in case of custom-duty cancellation. On November 13 Federal Assembly of Czech and Slovak Republics passed the Constitution Act on Federation Property Division and its Transfer on the Republics. This was based upon the territorial principle and the ratio 2:1 (in favour of the Czech Republic), complement by historical aspects. On November 25, 1992 Federal Assembly passed the Constitution Act on Extinction of the Czech and Slovak Federal Republic (ČSFR) to December 31, 1992. On December 16, 1992 the Czech National Council accepted the Constitution of the Czech Republic. On December 31, 1993 government of the Czech and

121

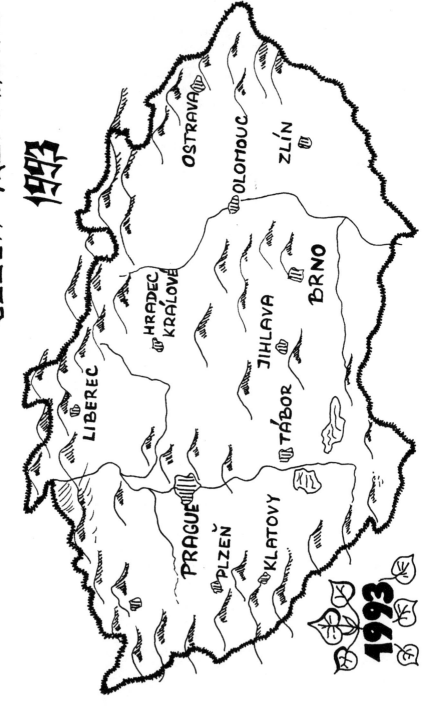

Slovak Federal Republic stopped its activities. On January 1, 1993 two independent States arose from federal Czechoslovakia, i.e. the Czech Republic and the Slovak Republic respectively.

1993 -
VÁCLAV HAVEL,
President
of the Czech Republic

On January 26, 1993 Václav Havel elected President of the Czech Republic. On February 2, 1993 inauguration of the first Czech President Václav Havel in Vladislav's Hall of Prague Castle took place. On February 4 - 7, 1993 exchange of hitherto valid federal banknotes for stamped ones (in nominal values 100, 500, 1 000 Czech crowns). On February 8, 1993 currency separation was put to an end. Thus, the Czechoslovak crown split in two independent currencies. In the course of July - November 1993 all of the stamped banknotes became valid. The same refers, in the same period of time, to all Federal coins as well. Both the banknotes and coins were exchanged in the new currency of the Czech Republic in a ratio 1:1. On January 1, 1994 Czech Republic became member of United Nations Security Council for as long as two years' time. On March 10, 1994 Czech Republic joined officially the Partnership for Peace.

January 7, 1993 Federal banknote stamping started.

January 19, 1993 Czech Republic became United Nations member.

February 4 - 7, 1993 Banknote exchange for stamped ones took place in Slovakia simultaneously with the Czech Republic.

February 15, 1993 Michal Kováč elected President of Slovakia.

March 2, Inauguration of the Slovak President M. Kováč took place.

December 8, 1993 Registrations of the second wave of Coupon privatization put to an end. Over 5.5 million of Czech citizens registered.

February 4, 1994 Television Nova started broadcasting.

*

Prague

APPENDIX

SOVEREIGNS AND STATE HEADS
OF NEIGHBOURING COUNTRIES

ROMAN REALM

KINGS OF GERMANY, EMPERORS OF ROME

Ludvig the German	826 - 876	(since 826 King of Bavaria, since 843 King of East Franconia)
Karloman	876 - 880	(King of Bavaria)
Ludvig III	876 - 882	(King of East Franconia)
Karl III, the Thick	876 - 888	(King of Franconia, since 879 King of Italy, since 881 Emperor of Rome, since 882 King of East Franconia)
Arnulf	887 - 899	(King of East Franconia, since 896 Emperor)
Ludvig IV, the Infant	900 - 911	(King of East Franconia)
Konrad I	911 - 918	
Heinrich I	919 - 936	
Otto I	936 - 973	(since 962 Emperor)
Otto II	961 - 983	(since 967 Emperor)
Otto III	983 - 1002	(since 996 Emperor)
Heinrich II	1002 - 1024	(since 1014 Emperor)
Konrad II	1024 - 1039	(since 1027 Emperor)
Heinrich III	1039 - 1056	(since 1046 Emperor)
Heinrich IV	1056 - 1105	(dethroned; since 1084 Emperor)
Rudolph the Schwab	1077 - 1080	
Hermann of Luxemburg	1081 - 1088	(gave up his throne)
Konrad, son of Heinrich IV	1087 - 1093	(dethroned)
Heinrich V	1106 - 1125	(since 1111 Emperor)
Lothar (III)	1125 - 1137	(since 1133 Emperor)
Konrad III	1138 - 1152	
Heinrich, son of Konrad III	1147 - 1150	
Friedrich I Barbarossa	1152 - 1190	(since 1155 Emperor)
Heinrich VI	1169 - 1197	(since 1191 Emperor)
Philip	1198 - 1208	
Otto IV	1198 - 1218	(since 1209 Emperor)
Friedrich II	1212 - 1250	(since 1220 Emperor)
Heinrich, son of Friedrich II	1222 - 1242	
Heinrich Raspe	1246 - 1247	
Konrad IV	1250 - 1254	

Wilhelm of Holland	1248 - 1256	
Richard of Cornwall	1257 - 1272	
Alphonse of Castilia	1257 - 1284	
Rudolph I of Habsburg	1273 - 1291	
Adolf of Nassavia	1292 - 1298	
Albrecht I	1298 - 1308	
Heinrich VII	1308 - 1313	(since 1312 Emperor)
Friedrich der Schöne	1314 - 1330	
Ludvig Bavarian	1314 - 1347	(since 1328 Emperor)
Karel IV of Luxemburg	1346 - 1378	(since 1355 Emperor)
Günther of Schwarzburg	1349	
Václav IV of Luxemburg	1376 - 1400	(dethroned)
Ruprecht of Palatinate	1400 - 1410	
Jošt of Moravia	1410 - 1411	
Zikmund of Luxemburg	1410 - 1437	(since 1433 Emperor)
Albrecht II	1438 - 1439	
Friedrich III	1440 - 1493	(since 1452 Emperor)
Maximilian I	1486 - 1519	(since 1508 Emperor)
Karl V	1519 - 1556	(since 1530 Emperor; gave up the throne)
Ferdinand I	1531 - 1564	(since 1556 Emperor)
Maximilian II	1562 - 1576	(since 1564 Emperor)
Rudolph II	1576 - 1612	(since 1576 Emperor)
Mathias	1612 - 1619	
Ferdinand II	1619 - 1637	
Ferdinand III	1637 - 1657	(since 1637 Emperor)
Leopold I	1658 - 1705	(since 1658 Emperor)
Joseph I	1705 - 1711	(since 1705 Emperor)
Karl VI	1711 - 1740	(since 1711 Emperor)
Karl VII of Bavaria	1740 - 1745	(since 1742 Emperor)
Franz I	1745 - 1765	(since 1745 Emperor)
Joseph II	1765 - 1790	(since 1765 Emperor)
Leopold II	1790 - 1792	(since 1790 Emperor)
Franz II	1792 - 1806	(since 1792 Emperor, gave up the throne, further on see Empire of Austria)

GERMANY

GERMAN EMPIRE

Vilhelm I	1871 - 1888
Friedrich III	1888
Vilhelm II	1888 - 1918

GERMAN REPUBLIC

Friedrich Ebert	1919 - 1925	(President)
Paul von Hindenburg	1925 - 1934	(President)

GREAT GERMAN REICH

Adolf Hitler	1934 - 1945	(Führer and Reich Chancellor)

GERMAN DEMOCRATIC REPUBLIC

Wilhelm Pieck	1949 - 1960	(President)
Walter Ulbricht	1960 - 1973	(Head of State Council)
Willi Stoph	1973 - 1976	(Head of State Council)
Erich Honecker	1976 - 1989	(Head of State Council)
Egon Krenz	1989	(Head of State Council)

FEDERAL REPUBLIC OF GERMANY

Theodor Heuss	1949 - 1959	(President)
Heinrich Lübke	1959 - 1969	(President)
Gustav Heinemann	1969 - 1974	(President)
Walter Scheel	1974 - 1979	(President)
Karl Carstens	1979 - 1984	(President)
Richard von Weizsäcker	1984 - 1994	(President)
Roman Herzog	1994 -	(President)

AUSTRIA

Margraves

Leopold I.	976 - 994
Heinrich I.	994 - 1018
Adalbert	1018 - 1055
Ernst	1055 - 1075
Leopold II.	1075 - 1095
Leopold III. (Saint)	1095 - 1136
Leopold IV.	1136 - 1141

Dukes

Heinrich II	1141 - 1177	(since 1156 Duke)
Leopold V	1177 - 1194	
FriedrichI	1195 - 1198	
Leopold VI	1198 - 1230	
Friedrich II	1230 - 1246	
Hermann of Baden	1247 - 1250	
Přemysl Otakar II	1251 - 1276	
Rudolph I	1276 - 1282	(King of Rome as well)
Albrecht I	1283 - 1308	(King of Rome as well)
Friedrich	1308 - 1330	(King of Rome as well)
Albert II	1330 - 1358	
Rudolph IV	1358 - 1365	
Albrecht III	1365 - 1395	
Albrecht IV	1395 - 1404	
Albrecht V (as Emperor A. II)	1404 - 1439	(since 1438 King of Rome and Bohemia)
Ladislav Pohrobek	1439 - 1457	(also King of Bohemia)
Friedrich V (as Emperor F. ИI)	1457 - 1493	(since 1440 King of Rome)
Maximilian I	1493 - 1519	(also King of Rome)
Ferdinand I	1519 - 1564	(also King of Bohemia and Hungary and, since 1556 Emperor of Rome)
Maximilian II	1564 - 1576	(also King of Bohemia, Hungary, Emp. of Rome)
Rudolph II	1576 - 1612	(also King of Bohemia, Hungary, Emp. of Rome)
Mathias	1612 - 1619	(also King of Bohemia, Hungary, Emp. of Rome)
Ferdinand II	1619 - 1637	(also King of Bohemia, Hungary, Emp. of Rome)
Ferdinand III	1637 - 1657	(also King of Bohemia, Hungary, Emp. of Rome)
Leopold I	1657 - 1705	(also King of Bohemia, Hungary, Emp. of Rome)
Joseph I	1705 - 1711	(also King of Bohemia, Hungary, Emp. of Rome)
Karl VI	1711 - 1740	(also King of Bohemia, Hungary, Emp. of Rome)
Maria Theresia	1740 - 1780	(also Queen of Bohemia, Hungary, Emp. of Rome)
Joseph II	1780 - 1790	(also King of Bohemia, Hungary, Emp. of Rome)
Leopold II	1790 - 1792	(also King of Bohemia, Hungary, Emp. of Rome)

EMPIRE OF AUSTRIA

Franz I (as Emperor of Rome Franz II)	1792 - 1835	(also King of Bohemia and Hungary and, up to 1806 Emp. of Rome, up to 1804 Emp. of Austria)
Ferdinand I	1835 - 1848	(Emp. of Austria, King of Bohemia and Hungary)
Franz Joseph I	1848 - 1916	(Emp. of Austria, King of Bohemia and Hungary)
Karl I	1916 - 1918	(Emp. of Austria, King of Bohemia and Hungary)

AUSTRIAN REPUBLIC

Presidents

Karl Seitz	1918 - 1920	(Head of State as President of National Assembly)
Michael Hainisch	1920 - 1928	
Wilhelm Miklas	1928 - 1938	
Annexion to Nazi Germany	1938 - 1945	
Karl Renner	1945 - 1950	
Theodor Körner	1951 - 1957	
Adolf Schärf	1957 - 1965	
Franz Jonas	1965 - 1974	
Rudolf Kirchschläger	1974 - 1986	
Kurt Waldheim	1986 - 1992	
Thomas Klestil	od r. 1992	

HUNGARY

Kings

Gejza	972 - 997	
Stephen I the Saint	997 - 1038	(since 1000 King)
Peter	1038 - 1041	
Samuel Aba	1041 - 1044	
Peter	1044 - 1046	
Andrew I	1046 - 1061	
Béla I	1061 - 1063	
Solomon	1063 - 1074	
Gejza I	1074 - 1077	
Ladislav I	1077 - 1095	
Koloman	1095 - 1114	
Stephen II	1114 - 1131	
Béla II	1131 - 1141	
Gejza II	1141 - 1161	
Stephen III	1161 - 1162	

Ladislav II	1162	
Stephen IV	1162	
Stephen III	1162 - 1173	
Béla III	1173 - 1196	
Emerich	1196 - 1204	
Ladislav III	1204 - 1205	
Andrew II	1205 - 1235	
Béla IV	1235 - 1270	
Stephen V	1270 - 1272	
Ladislav IV	1272 - 1290	
Andrew III	1290 - 1301	
Ladislav V	1301 - 1305	(Václav III, King of Bohemia)
Ota	1305 - 1308	
Charles Robert	1308 - 1342	
Louis I	1342 - 1382	(since 1370 also King of Poland)
Mary	1382 - 1385	
Charles III	1385 - 1387	
Zikmund of Luxemburg	1387 - 1437	(also Emperor of Rome and King of Bohemia)
Albrecht of Habsburg	1437 - 1439	(also King of Rome and Bohemia)
Elisabeth	1439 - 1440	
Vladislav of Jagello	1440 - 1444	(also King of Poland)
Ladislav	1444 (1453) - 1457	(also King of Bohemia)
Jan Hunyady	1444 - 1453	(Regent of the kingdom)
Matthew Korwin	1458 - 1490	
Vladislav of Jagello	1490 - 1516	(also King of Bohemia)
Louis II	1516 - 1526	(also King of Bohemia)
Jan Zápolský	1526 - 1540	(in feud with Ferdinand)
Ferdinand I	1526 - 1564	(also Emperor of Rome and King of Bohemia)
Maximilian II	1564 - 1576	(also Emperor of Rome and King of Bohemia)
Rudolph II	1576 - 1608	(also Emperor of Rome and King of Bohemia)
Matthew	1608 - 1619	(also Emperor of Rome and King of Bohemia)
Ferdinand II	1619 - 1637	(also Emperor of Rome and King of Bohemia)
Ferdinand III	1637 - 1657	(also Emperor of Rome and King of Bohemia)
Ferdinand IV	1647 - 1654	
Leopold I	1657 - 1705	(also Emperor of Rome and King of Bohemia)
Joseph I	1705 - 1711	(also Emperor of Rome and King of Bohemia)
Charles VI	1711 - 1740	(also Emperor of Rome and King of Bohemia)
Maria Theresia	1740 - 1780	(also Empress of Rome and Queen of Bohemia)
Joseph II	1780 - 1790	(also Emperor of Rome)
Leopold II	1790 - 1792	(also Emperor of Rome and King of Bohemia)
Franz II	1792 - 1835	(also Emperor of Rome and King of Bohemia; since 1804 Emperor of Austria)

Ferdinand V	1835 - 1848	(also Emperor of Austria and King of Bohemia)
Franz Joseph I	1848 - 1916	(also Emperor of Austria and King of Bohemia)
Karl	1916 - 1918	(also Emperor of Austria and King of Bohemia)

HUNGARY - REPUBLIC OF HUNGARY - PEOPLE'S REPUBLIC OF HUNGARY

Michael Károlyi	1918 - 1919	(President)
Hungarian Republic of Councils	1919	
Miklós Horthy	1919 - 1944	(Regent)
Zoltán Tildy	1946 - 1949	(President of Hungarian Republic)
Árpád Szakasits	1949 - 1952	(President of the People's Republic of Hungary)
István Dobi	1952 - 1967	(Head of the Presidium of People's Rep. of Hung.)
Pál Losonczi	1967 - 1987	(Head of the Presidium of People's Rep. of Hung.)
Károly Németh	1987 - 1988	(Head of the Presidium of People's Rep. of Hung.)
Brunó Straub F.	1988 - 1989	(Head of the Presidium of People's Rep. of Hung.)
Mátyás Szürös	1989 - 1990	(President ad interim of People's Rep. of Hungary)
Árpád Göncz	1990	(President ad interim of People's Rep. of Hungary)
Árpád Göncz	od r. 1990	(President of Hungarian Republic)

POLAND

Knights

Mieszek I	960 (?) - 992	
Boleslav I, the Valiant	992 - 1025	(since 1025 King)
Mieszek II Lambert	1025 - 1034	(since 1025 King)
Kazimierz I, the Innovator	1034 - 1058	
Boleslav II, the Valiant	1058 - 1080	(since 1076 King)
Vladislav I Herzman	1079 - 1102	
Boleslav III	1102 - 1138	
Vladislav II	1138 - 1159	(? reigned until 1146)
Boleslav IV Curled	1146 - 1173	
Mieszek III, the Old	1173 - 1177	
Kazimierz II, the Just	1177 - 1194	

Mieszek III, the Old	1194 - 1202
Vladislav III	1202 - 1206
Leszek, the White	1206 - 1227
Boleslav, the Bashful	1227 - 1279
Leszek, the Black	1279 - 1288

Kings

Przemysl II of Great Poland	1295 - 1296	
Václav II, the Czech	1300 - 1305	
Vladislav I Lokietek	1306 - 1333	(coronated 1320)
Kazimierz III, the Great	1333 - 1370	
Louis I of Anjou	1370 - 1382	(since 1342 King of Hungary)
Hedwiga	1383 - 1386	

Vladislav II Jagello	1386 - 1434
Vladislav III	1434 - 1444
Kazimierz IV	1445 - 1492
Jan Albrecht	1492 - 1501
Alexander I	1501 - 1506
Sigismund I, the Old	1506 - 1548
Sigismund II Augustus	1548 - 1572

Henry of Valois	1573 - 1574
Stephen Bathory	1575 - 1586

Sigismund III Vasa	1587 - 1632
Vladislav IV	1632 - 1648
Jan II Kazimierz	1648 - 1668
Michael Korybut Wiśniowiecki	1669 - 1673
Jan III Sobieski	1674 - 1696
Augustus II, the Saxonian	1697 - 1706
Stanislav Leszczyński	1704 - 1710
Augustus II, the Saxonian	1710 - 1733
Stanislav Leszczyński	1733 - 1734
Augustus III	1734 - 1763
Stanislav Augustus Poniatowski	1764 - 1795

POLISH REPUBLIC - PEOPLE'S REPUBLIC OF POLAND

Presidents

Józef Pilsudski	1918 - 1922	(Head of the State)
Gabriel Narutowicz	1922	
Stanislav Wojciechowski	1922 - 1926	
Ignacy Mościcki	1926 - 1939	

Occupation Period (Government General)	1939 - 1944	
Boleslav Bierut	1943 - 1952	(Head of Provincial National Council; since 1947 President of the Republic)
Aleksander Zawadzki	1952 - 1964	(Head of State Council)
Edward Ochab	1964 - 1968	(Head of State Council)
Marian Spychalski	1968 - 1970	
Józef Cyrankiewicz	1970 - 1972	
Henryk Jabloński	1972 - 1985	(Head of State Council)
Wojciech Jaruzelski	1985 - 1989	(Head of State Council)
Wojciech Jaruzelski	1989 - 1990	(President)
Lech Wałesa	od r. 1990	(President)

POPES

Hadrianus I	771 - 795	
Leo III	795 - 816	
Stephen V	816 - 817	
Paschalus I	817 - 824	
Eugenius II	824 - 827	
Valentinus	827	
Gregory IV	827 - 844	
Sergius II	844 - 847	
Leo IV	847 - 855	
Benedictus III	855 - 858	
Nicolas I	858 - 867	
Hadrianus II	867 - 872	
Joannes VIII	872 - 882	
Marinus I	882 - 884	
Hadrianus III	884 - 885	
Stephen VI	885 - 891	
Formosus	891 - 896	
Bonipfacius VI	896	
Stephen VII	896 - 897	(banished)

Romanus	897 - 898	
Theodorus II	898	
Joannes IX	898 - 900	
Benedictus IV	900 - 903	
Leo V	903	
Christophorus	903 - 904	(banished)
Sergius III	904 - 911	
Anastasius III	911 - 913	
Lando	913 - 914	
Joannes X	914 - 928	(dethroned)
Leo VI	928 - 929	
Stephen VIII	929 - 931	
Joannes XI	931 - 936	
Leo VII	936 - 939	
Stephen IX	939 - 942	
Marinus II (Martin III.)	942 - 946	
Agapitus II	946 - 955	
Joannes XII	955 - 963	(dethroned)
Leo VIII	963 - 965	
Benedictus V	964	(dethroned)
Joannes XIII	965 - 972	
Benedictus VI	973 - 974	
Boniphacius VII	974	(temporarily banished)
Benedictus VII	974 - 983	
Joannes XIV	983 - 984	
Boniphacius VII	984 - 985	(acends throne for the second time)
Joannes XV	985 - 996	
Gregory V	996 - 999	
Joannes XVI (counter-pope)	997 - 998	(dethroned)
Silvestr II (Gerbertus)	999 - 1003	
Joannes XVII (Secco)	1003	
Joannes XVIII (Phasianus)	1003 - 1009	
Sergius IV (Petrus)	1009 - 1012	
Benedictus VIII (Johannes)	1012 - 1024	
Gregory (counter-pope)	1012	
Joannes XIX	1024 - 1032	
Benedictus IX (Theophylactus)	1032 - 1045	(gave up the throne)
Silvestr III (counter-pope)	1045 - 1046	(dethroned)
Gregory VI (Johannes Gratianus)	1045 - 1046	(dethroned)
Clementus II	1046 - 1047	
Benedictus IX	1047 - 1048	(banished)
Damasus II (Poppo)	1047 - 1048	
Leo IX (Bruno Hugonis)	1048 - 1054	
Victor II (Gebhardus)	1054 - 1057	
Stephen X (Fridericus)	1057 - 1058	
Benedictus X (Joannes)	1058 - 1060	(dethroned)
Nicolas II (Gerhardus)	1058 - 1061	

Alexander II (Anselmus)	1061 - 1073	
Honorius II (Cadalus, counter-pope)	1061 - 1064	(dethroned)
Gregory VII (Hildebrandus)	1073 - 1085	
Climentus III (Wibertus, counter-pope)	1080 - 1100	
Victor III (Desiderius)	1086 - 1087	
Urbanus II (Odo de Castellione)	1088 - 1099	
Paschalus II (Reinerius)	1099 - 1118	
Theodoricus (counter-pope)	1100	(banished)
Albertus (counter-pope)	1102	(dethroned)
Silvester IV (Maginulfus, counter-pope)	1105 - 1111	(dethroned)
Gelasius II (Johannes Caietanus)	1118 - 1119	
Gregory VIII. (Burdinus, counter-pope)	1118 - 1121	(dethroned)
Calixtus II (Guido)	1119 - 1124	
Celestinus II (Thebaltus Buccapecus, counter-pope)	1124	(gave up the throne)
Honorius II (Lambertus de Fagniano)	1124 - 1130	
Innocensius II (Gregorius Parapeschi)	1130 - 1143	
Anacletus II (Petrus de Frangipanis, counter-pope)	1130 - 1138	
Victor IV (Gregorius, couznter-pope)	1138	(gave up the throne)
Celestinus II (Guido de Castello)	1143 - 1144	
Lucius II (Gerardus)	1144 - 1145	
Eugenius III (Petrus Bernardus)	1145 - 1153	
Anastasius IV (Conradus de Suburra)	1153 - 1154	
Hadrianus IV (Nicolaus Breakspear)	1154 - 1159	
Alexander III (Rolandus Bandinellus)	1159 - 1181	
Victor IV (Octavianus, counter-pope)	1159 - 1164	
Paschalus III (Quido Cremsis, counter-pope)	1164 - 1168	
Calixtus III (Johannes Struma, counter-pope)	1168 - 1178	(gave up the throne)
Innocencius III (Landus Sitinus, counter-pope)	1179 - 1180	(imprisoned)
Lucius III (Ubaldus Allucingulli)	1181 - 1185	
Urbanus III (Umbertus Cribellus)	1185 - 1187	
Gregory VIII (Albertus)	1187	
Clementus III (Paulus Scolarus)	1187 - 1191	
Celestinus III (Hyacinthus Bobo)	1191 - 1198	
Innocentius III (Lotharius Senensis)	1198 - 1216	
Honorius III (Cencius Sabellus)	1216 - 1227	
Gregory IX (Ugolinus Senensis)	1227 - 1241	
Celestinus IV (Guifredus Castellioneus)	1241	
Innocentius IV (Sinibaldus Fliscus)	1243 - 1254	
Alexander IV (Reinaldus Senensis)	1254 - 1261	
Urbanus IV (Jacobus Pantaleonis)	1261 - 1264	
Clementus IV (Guido Grossus)	1265 - 1268	
Gregory X (Theobaldus Visconti)	1271 - 1276	
Innocentius V (Petrus de Tarentasia)	1276	
Hadrian V (Otobonus Fliscus)	1276	
Joannes XXI (XX., Petrus Juliani)	1276 - 1277	
Nicolas III (Johannes Caietanus Ursinus)	1277 - 1280	
Martin IV (Simon Mompitius)	1281 - 1285	
Honorius IV (Jacobus Sabellus)	1285 - 1287	

Nicolas IV (Hieronymus Masci)	1288 - 1292	
Celestinus V (Petrus de Murrone)	1294	(gave up the throne)
Boniphatius VIII (Benedictus Caietanus)	1294 - 1303	
Benedictus XI (Nicolaus Bocasinus)	1303 - 1304	

SINCE 1309 IN AVIGNON

Clementus V (Bertrand de Gotto)	1305 - 1314	
Joannes XXII (XXI, Jacobus Arnaldi Deuza)	1316 - 1334	
Nicolas V (Petrus de Corbairia, counter-pope)	1328 - 1330	(gave up the throne)
Benedictus XII (Jacobus Furnarius)	1334 - 1342	
Clementus VI (Petrus Rogerii)	1342 - 1352	
Innocentius VI (Stephanus Alberti)	1352 - 1362	
Urbanus V (Guillelmus Grimoaldi)	1362 - 1370	
Gregory XI (Petrus Rogerii)	1370 - 1378	
Clementus VII (Robertus de Gebennis, counter-pope)	1378 - 1394	
Benedictus XIII (Petrus de Luna, counter-pope)	1394 - 1409	(dethroned by Council of Pisa; in 1417 dethroned by Council of Constance)

IN ROME

Urbanus VI (Bartholomeus Prignanus)	1378 - 1389	
Boniphacius IX (Petrus Tomacellus)	1389 - 1404	
Innocentius VII (Cosmus de Melioratis)	1404 - 1406	
Gregory XII (Angellus Corrarius)	1406 - 1409	(dethroned by Council of Pisa; in 1415 gave up the throne)

IN PISA

Alexander V (Petrus Philargus)	1409 - 1410	
Joannes XXIII (XXII, Balthasar Cossa)	1410 - 1415	(dethroned by Council of Constance)

IN ROME

Martin V (Otto Colonna)	1417 - 1431	
Clementus VIII (Egidius Munion, counter-pope)	1424 - 1429	(gave up the throne)
Eugenius IV (Gabriel Condolmieri)	1431 - 1439	(dethroned by Council of Basle)
Felix IV (Amadeo VII, Duke of Saavoie, counter-pope)	1439 - 1449	(gave up the throne)
Nicolas V (Thomas Parentucelli)	1447 - 1455	
Calixtus III (Alphonsus Borgia)	1455 - 1458	
Pius II (Eneas Silvius Piccolomini)	1458 - 1464	
Paul II (Pietro Barbo)	1464 - 1471	
Sixtus IV (Francesco della Rovere)	1471 - 1484	
Innocentius VIII (Johannes Bapt. Zibo)	1484 - 1492	
Alexander VI (Roderigo Borgia)	1492 - 1503	

Pius III (Francesco Piccolomini)	1503
Julius II (Giuliano della Rovere)	1503 - 1513
Leo X (Giovanni Medici)	1513 - 1521
Hadrian VI (Adriano Florentino)	1522 - 1523
Clementus VII (Giulio Medici)	1523 - 1534
Paul III (Alessandro Farnese)	1534 - 1549
Julius III (Giovanni Maria del Monte)	1550 - 1555
Marcellus II (Marceli Cervino)	1555
Paul IV (Gian Pietro Caraffa)	1555 - 1559
Pius IV (Giovanni Angelo Medici)	1559 - 1565
Pius V (Michele Ghislieri)	1566 - 1572
Gregory XIII (Ugo Buoncompagni)	1572 - 1585
Sixtus V (Felice Peretti)	1585 - 1590
Urbanus VII (Giambattista Castagna)	1590
Gregory XIV (Nicolao Sfondrati)	1590 - 1591
Innocentius IX (Gian Antonio Facchinetti)	1591
Clementus VIII (Hyppolyto Aldobrandini)	1592 - 1605
Leo XI (Alessandro Medici)	1605
Paul V (Camillo Borghese)	1605 - 1621
Gregory XV (Alessandro Ludovisi)	1621 - 1623
UrbanusVIII (Maffeo Barberini)	1623 - 1644
Innocetius X (Giambattista Pamfili)	1644 - 1655
Alexander VII (Fabio Chigi)	1655 - 1667
Clementus IX (Giulio Rospigliosi)	1667 - 1669
Clementus X (Emilio Altieri)	1670 - 1676
Innocentius XI (Benedetto Odescalchi)	1676 - 1689
Alexander VIII (Pietro Ottoboni)	1689 - 1691
Innocentius XII (Antonio Pignatelli)	1691 - 1700
Clementus XI (Giovanni Franc. Albani)	1700 - 1721
Innocentius XIII (Michelangelo de Conti)	1721 - 1724
Benedictus XIII (Pietro Franc. Orsini)	1724 - 1730
Clementus XII (Lorenzo Corsini)	1730 - 1740
Benedictus XIV (Prospero Lambertini)	1740 - 1758
Clementus XIII (Carlo Rezzonico)	1758 - 1769
Clementus XIV (Giovanni Antonio Ganganelli)	1769 - 1774
Pius VI (Giovanni Angello Braschi)	1775 - 1799
Pius VII (Gregorio Barnaba Chiaramonti)	1800 - 1823
Leo XII (Annibale della Genga)	1823 - 1829
Pius VIII (Francisco Xav. Castiglione)	1829 - 1830
Gregory XVI (Mauro Capellari)	1831 - 1846
Pius IX (Giovanni Maria Mastai Feretti)	1846 - 1878
Leo XIII (Gioachino Pecci)	1878 - 1903
Pius X (Giuseppe Sarto)	1903 - 1914
Benedictus XV (Giacomo della Chiesa)	1914 - 1922
Pius XI (Achille Ratti)	1922 - 1939
Pius XII (Eugenio Pacelli)	1939 - 1958
Joannes XXIII (Angello Giuseppe Roncalli)	1958 - 1963
Paul VI (Giovanni Battista Montini)	1963 - 1978

Joannes Paul I (Albino Luciani)   1978
Joannes Paul II (Karol Wojtyła)   od r. 1978

GOVERNMENTS OF THE HABSBURG MONARCHY WITHIN THE PERIOD 1848 - 1867

PRIME MINISTERS

1848	Count Franz Kolowrat - Liebsteinsky	(President of Min. Council since March 20)
	Count Karl Ficquelmount	(President of Min.Council since April 18)
1848	Franz v. Pillersdorf	(President of Min. Council since May 8)
	Anton v. Doblhoff-Dier	(President of Min. Council since July 8)
1848	Johann F. v. Wessenberg	(President of Min. Council since July 18)
1848 - 1852	Knight Felix Schwarzenberg	
1852 - 1859	Alexander Bach	(provisory President of Min. Conference April 9, 1852 - April 11, 1952)
	Count Carl F. Buol-Schaunstein	(President of Min. Conference since April 11, 1852)
	Count Johann B. Rechberg -Rothenlöwen	(President of Min. Conference since May 17, 1859)
1859 - 1861	count Johann B. Rechberg	(President of Min. Conference)
1861 - 1865	Archduke Rainer	(President of Min. Conference)
	hr. Mensdorff-Pouilly	(President of Min. Conference, since June 26, 1865)
1865 - 1867	hr. Richard Belcredi	(President of Min. Conference)

GOVERNMENTS OF PŘEDLITAVSKO WITHIN THE PERIOD 1867 - 1918

PRIME MINISTERS

1867	Friedrich F. Beust	
	Count Eduard Taaffe	
1867 - 1870	Knight Carlos Auersperg	
	Count Eduard Taaffe	(since 1868)
1870	Leopold v. Hasner	
1870 - 1871	Count Alfred Potocki	
1871	Count Karl Hohenwart	
1871	Ludvig v. Holzgethan	
1871 - 1879	Knight Adolf Auersperg	
1879	Karl v. Stremayr	
1879 - 1893	Count Eduard Taaffe	
1893 - 1895	Knight Alfred Windischgrätz	
1895	Count Erich Kielmansegg	
1895 - 1897	Count Kazimir Badeni	
1897 - 1898	Paul v. Gautsch	

1898 - 1899	Count Franz Thun	
1899 - 1900	Count Manfred Clary-Aldringen	
	Heinrich v. Wittek	(provisory since 1899)
1900 - 1904	Ernst v. Koerber	
1905 - 1906	Paul v. Gautsch	
1906	princ Konrad Hohenlohe-Schillingsfürst	
1906 - 1908	Max. W. v. Beck	
1908 - 1911	Count Richard Bienerth	
1911	Paul v. Gautsch	
1911 - 1916	Count Karl Stürgkh	(since May 15 - September 14 1912 substituted by K. von Heinold, Home Office Secretary)
1916	Ernst v. Koerberg	
1916 - 1917	Count Heinrich Clam-Martinic	
1917 - 1918	Ernst v. Seidler	
1918	Max v. Hussarek	
1918	Heinrich Lammasch	

HUNGARIAN GOVERNMENTS WITHIN THE PERIOD 1948 - 1918

PRIME MINISTERS

1848	Count Ludvig Batthyány	
1848 - 1849	National Defence Committee headed by Ludvig Kossuth	
1849	Bartholomew Szemere	
1849 - 1860	Hungary non-independent	
1860 - 1867	Period of constitutional experiments	
1867 - 1871	Count Julius Andrássy	
1871 - 1872	Count Melchior Lónyay	
1872 - 1874	Joseph Szlávy	
1874 - 1875	Stefan Bittó	
1875 - 1890	Baronet Vojtěch v. Wenckheim	
	Koloman Tisza	(took over the Cabinet since October 20, 1875)
1890 - 1892	Count Julius Szapáry	
1892 - 1895	AlexanderWekerle	
1895 - 1899	Baron Dezider Bánffy	
1899 - 1903	Koloman Széll	
1903	Count Karl Khuen-Héderváry	
1903 - 1905	Count Stefan Tisza	
1905 - 1906	Baronet Gejza v. Fejérváry	
1906 - 1910	Alexander Wekerle	
1910 - 1912	Count Karl Khuen-Héderváry	
1912 - 1913	Ladislav v. Lukács	
1913 - 1917	Count Stefan Tisza	

1917	Count Morris Esterházy
1917 - 1918	Alexander Wekerle
1918	Count Michael Károlyi

GOVERNMENTS OF THE CZECHOSLOVAK REPUBLIC WITHIN THE PERIOD 1918 - 1938

PRIME MINISTERS

1918 - 1919	Karel Kramář	
1919 - 1920	Vlastimil Tusar	
1920	Vlastimil Tusar	
1920 - 1921	Jan Černý	(State Service government)
1921 - 1922	Edvard Beneš	
1922 - 1925	Antonín Švehla	
1925 - 1926	Antonín Švehla	
1926	Jan Černý	(State service government)
1926 - 1929	Antonín Švehla	
1929	František Udržal	
1929 - 1932	František Udržal	
1932 - 1934	Jan Malypetr	
1934 - 1935	Jan Malypetr	
1935	Jan Malypetr	
1935	Milan Hodža	
1935 - 1937	Milan Hodža	
1937 - 1938	Milan Hodža	
1938	Jan Syrový General of the Army	(State Service government)

CENTRAL GOVERNMENTS OF POST-MUNICH CZECHOSLOVAKIA

PRIME MINISTERS

| 1938 | Jan Syrový General of the Army | (State Service government) |
| 1938 - 1939 | Rudolf Beran | |

AUTONOMOUS GOVERNMENTS OF SLOVAKIA

PRIME MINISTERS

| 1938 | Jozef Tiso |

1938 - 1939	Jozef Tiso
1939	Jozef Tiso
1939	Jozef Sivák
1939	Karol Sidor

AUTONOMOUS GOVERNMENTS OF CARPATHO-RUSSIA

PRIME MINISTERS

1938	Andrej Bródy
1938	Augustin Voloshin
1938 - 1939	Augustin Voloshin
1939	Augustin Voloshin

PROTECTORATE GOVERNMENTS

PRIME MINISTERS

1939	Rudolf Beran	(continuation of the Czecho-Slovak Post-Munich government without K. Sidor)
1939 - 1942	Aloi Eliáš Division General	
1942 - 1945	Jaroslav Krejčí	
1945	Richard Bienert	

GOVERNMENTS OF THE SLOVAK REPUBLIC

PRIME MINISTERS

1939	Jozef Tiso
1939 - 1944	Vojtěch Tuka
1944 - 1945	Štefan Tiso

CZECHOSLOVAK GOVERNMENTS IN EXILE

PRIME MINISTERS

1940 - 1942	Jan Šrámek
1942 - 1945	Jan Šrámek

CZECHOSLOVAK GOVERNMENTS WITHIN THE PERIOD 1945 - 1968

PRIME MINISTERS

1945	Zdeněk Ferlinger	
1945 - 1946	Zdeněk Ferlinger	
1946 - 1948	Klement Gottwald	
1948	Klement Gottwald	
1948 - 1954	Antonín Zápotocký	
	Viliam Široký	(since March 21, 1953)
1954 - 1960	Viliam Široký	
1960 - 1963	Viliam Široký	
1963 - 1968	Jozef Lenárt	
1968	Oldřich Černík	

CZECHOSLOVAK FEDERAL GOVERNMENTS WITHIN THE PERIOD 1969 - 1989

PRIME MINISTERS

1969	Oldřich Černík	
1969 - 1971	Oldřich Černík	(up to January 28, 1970)
	Lubomír Štrougal	(since January 28, 1970)
1971 - 1976	Lubomír Štrougal	
1976 - 1981	Lubomír Štrougal	
1981 - 1986	Lubomír Štrougal	
1986 - 1988	Lubomír Štrougal	
1988 - 1989	Ladislav Adamec	

CZECHOSLOVAK FEDERAL GOVERNMENTS WITHIN THE PERIOD 1989 - 1992

PRIME MINISTERS

1989 - 1990	Marián Čalfa	
1990 - 1992	Marián Čalfa	
1992	Jan Stráský	(since July 2, 1992 until the end the Federation Dec. 31, 1992)

CZECH GOVERNMENT SINCE 1992

PRIME MINISTER

since 1992	Václav Klaus	(since July 2, 1992 Czech government appointed together with the last federal government)

Note: The appendix was elaborated on the basis of informations acquired from the publication "Czechoslovak History in Dates, Publisher Svoboda, Prague 1986 and complemented by contemporary items.

ARCHITECTURAL STYLES
IN CZECH COUNTRIES

Almost all of the architectural styles known to Europe have been used during the past centuries in Czech countries. The earliest architectural monuments areė the religious ones, such as chapels, churches and monasteries. Also from later periods, secular monuments, such as strongholds, citadels, castles and urban buildings have remained preserved.

GREAT MORAVIA

The earliest of our architectural monuments date from the pre-Romanesque period. The remnants of the latter were discovered by archaeologists upon the territory of Great Moravia, e.g. rotunda and church of Mikulčice, church of Sady, not far from Uherské Hradiště. Great-Moravian churches were made of stone, both innerly and outerly plastered, painted and roofed with burnt files. Their reconstructions are carried out according to standing churches of equal ground-plans abroad.

ROMANCE (ROMANESQUE) STYLE

This style had its rise in countries belonging to the Roman Empire already gone in those times. The name is derived from Latin Rome. There, stone architecture had already had its tradition of hundreds of years. Gradually this art spread, in all its forms, all over Europe and other countries as well.

In Czech countries, the Romanesque style started developing after 1100, and culminates in the first half of the 13th century. The Romanesque style is marked by its massiveness and relatively little pronounced diversity and loftiness, all of the monuments, as well as individual elements irradiate heaviness. Window and door openings are small (with semi-circular archs), the wings opening on either side to ensure better illumination. The most characteristic feature of the outer wall diversity is the so-called arch frieze beneath the main cornice. From among the most important Romanesque monuments of our country to be mentioned are fortified, castles Roudnice and Přimda, rotunda in Znojmo, on the Řip mountain, Saint George's Basilica at the Prague Castle, monasteries Strahov and Sázava.

GOTHIC STYLE

The main features of this style are (simplified) broken arch, rib vault, supporting system, perpendicular line and form slenderness pointing upwards. The Gothic architecture was complemented by plastic details adorned with figural, animal and plant themes and paintings (not pictures only).

In our countries the Gothic style was used approximately since the second half of the 13th century until the end of the 15th century. The most remarquable Gothic monuments are Karlštejn, Zvíkov, Bezděz (castles); Mladá Boleslav, New City of Prague, St. Vitus's Cathedral in Prague, St. Bartholomew's in Kolín, St. Barbara's in Kutná Hora, municipal buildings such as Old Town-Hall, Bridge Towers close by Charles's Bridge, Powder Gate in Prague and the like.

RENNAISSANCE

This style's cradle is Italy. Rennaissance, in Italian "rinascita" means "new birth", "revival" of the ancient, classical culture. The Rennaissance architecture is impressive due to its statically peaceful stratification of horizontal stages occasionally separated by cornices. This impression is still emphasized by the attic, i.e. the typically Rennaissance concluding element over the main cornice. The Rennaissance style is characterized by joint windows in a common frame. In Rennaissance arcades the so-called order superiority ranged from the simplest and most compact columns (or pillars) in the ground-floor up to increasingly slender and adorned ones in the stages. The front is flat. Architectural plasticity of the walls is accentuated by paintings or sgrafitti. The sgrafitto technique consists in the application of a two-layer plaster, whose upper (light) layer is, in a moist state, scratched off to reach the lower (dark), dried up one. Another contribution of the Rennaissance style is the commical balustrade appearing in the arcade parapet.

The Rennaissance dominates the architecture of our countries up to the beginning of the 17th century. As a prevailing feature may well be considered the effort of making the environment more agreeable and comfortable. That is why numerous noblemen's mansions, such as those of Litomyšl, Telč, Velké Losiny; palaces, such as Schwarzenberg's, Maritinic's; summer-residences, such as Hvězda on Bílá Hora, Queen Ann's Belvedere at Prague castle, municipal houses (Telč, Tábor) were constructed. In this period, religious monuments are relatively rare.

BAROQUE AND ROCOCO

BAROQUE STYLE

Baroque style developed in Italy in the 16th century and spread gradually all over Europe. In our countries, the post-Bílá Horá period, the Baroque style was applied to an increasingly large extent. The process started at about the beginning of the 17th up to first half of the 18th century. The early Baroque prefers straight lines and rectangularity on façades and ground-plans of buildings, the top Baroque, however, has more curves; the spaces appear as if composed of mutually penetrating cylinders and other bodies. The walls show bends and waves, the ground-plan consisting of ellipses, concave and convex forms. Thus, the space composition becomes vague. Domes and windows are intended to let the light artfully enter the church spaces. This is purposely underlined by wide-stretched frescoes evoking illusion of widening space and opening sights of overcast heaven. The over-all impression is accentuated by gold, stucco and artificial marble. Frequently, it is all designed to produce an outer effect, prevalently. Lots of vaults are actually false, board-panelled and outerly covered with plaster, strucco and paintings. The main characteristic of Baroque is the adaptation to surrounding sites, as well as its opulent sculptural adornment (Kuks in East Bohemia).

Among significant Baroque monuments to be mentioned are Klementinum in Prague, Svatý Kopeček near Olomouc, Saint Nicholas's churches in the Old Town and Lesser Town in Prague, mansions of Lobkovice, Černín, Valdstein of Prague, Roudnice, Chlumec nad Cidlinou, Mnichovo Hradiště and the like.

ROCOCO

The last era, or rather the late Baroque episode, is Rococo, its most remarkable feature being the rocaic ornament. As a matter of fact, Rococo is to be looked upon as diminuated Baroque. Rococo is prevalently applied to adorn interiors of buildings (Hořín u Mělníka). In our countries Rococo was in vogue since the second half of the forties up to the éseventies of the 18th century.

CLASSICISM

Classicism is inspired by the traditions of ancient Greece and Rome. First, it reminds one of Baroque outerly, it is however, more sever at abandoning motility of forms and ground-plans, the façades getting flat, the details dry with increasing diversity of geometry. On buildings, main fabion cornices started making its appearance. On gables, window cornices as well as portal openings compressing semieliptical arches became frequent. Triangle gables and column orders prove to be quite abundant, such as Corinth order, composed order and, partly, Ionic order as well. Quite popular motifs are medals with reliefed profiles of Roman emperors surrounded by leaf rolls.

In Czech countries Classicism was in vogue in the architecture since the eighties of the 18th up to the beginning of the 19th centuries. The remarkable classicist monuments of our country belong to Bertramka in Prague, watering-places of Teplice, Mariánské Lázně and Františkovy Lázně, Estate Theatre in Prague, citadels of Josefov, Terezín and the like.

EMPIRE

Empire derives its name from French empire, Latin imperium. This style was mostly popular in the period of time, when Napoleon Bonaparte proclaimed himself emperor in 1804 and moreover, throughout the first half of the 19th century. Empire is considered not to differ much from classicism, taking over from the antique Greek architecture the earliest style, i.e. the Dorsique order, but using the Ionic one as well. Cornices with brackets, capitals but the columns themselves would sometimes be made of a whitewashed wood the same way as façades. Cast iron, from which various elements such a Dorsic columns, railings, gratings, crosses and the like are cast became the new material. Characteristic triangular gables with tympanons, sometimes complemented by stucco plasters, inscriptions with eras or broken semi-circular or segmented windows are used. Church tower helmets (often four-sided ones only) are plain pyramids. Empire is applied to building municipal tenement houses (Platýz in Prague being considered the first), public baths, theaters, railroad stations, factories and the like. Kačina, not far from Kutná Hora, is one of the most beautiful Empire mansions.

ROMANTICISM

Romantic consideration of future, exotics of remote countries penetrated into all arts, including architecture, by the end of the 18th century. In architecture it culminated within the period 1790 - 1860 approximately. The nobility, thinking back to its past glory, turned toward the chivalrous Middle Ages. Its brilliance, seen from the romantic viewpoint, is to be reflected in expensive adaptations of older manorial mansions.

In Czech countries a wide-spread echo finds the English (Windsor) Neogothic style, characterized by blunt ends of buildings and towers and multisided corner turrets with toothed battlements. Another element is the Tudor arch used in portal gates, windows and rib vaults. The main representatives of the Romantic English (Windsor) Neogothic Style in mansion architecture are the castles Hluboká nad Vltavou (1841 - 1871) and Lednice in South Moravia (1843 - 1856). Many other buildings, such as town-halls, railroad stations, schools, barracks, factories, breweries, hospitals, tenement houses, bridges and the like have this representation also.

Another trend of Romanticism in Czech countries was inspired by French Gothic, whose castles and cylindrical, pointedly roofed towers and bulwarks remind us of Czech medieval feudal mansions to a considerably greater extent, Windsor Gothic. In this style the castles of Žleby not far from Čáslav and

Bouzov castle were reconstructed. Despite the outspoken effort to evoke impression of a medieval seat, the interiors of the latter remain 19 th century rooms.

HISTORICAL STYLES ERA

NEO-GOTHICS
NEO-ROMANESQUE
NEO-RENNAISSANCE
NEO-BAROQUE

The era of historical styles in architecture covers almost the whole of the second half of the 19th century reaching until the beginning of the 20th century. The contemporaneous development of technology, growing civic requirements aimed at all-dominating prosperity, rentability and usefulness, confront architecture and architects with big tasks. The development intensity seemed to have exceeded creative possibilities of the time. Since there was no time to experiment and to search for new ways, the historical styles offered themselves as a remedy. Historicism in architecture proves to be an era of conscious and purposeful imitation of past historical styles taken from non-Bohemian countries, as well. Since the fourties of the 19th century, Empire has been looked upon as a style quite sufficient for buildings and tenement houses only, whereas more important constructions soon clad themselves in historical styles. First of all, medieval i.e. Gothics and Romanesque styles were recommended for erection of churches. Next came Rennaissance, the most competent style for castles, town-halls and schools. By the very end of this era appeared the hitherto neglected and refused Baroque.

SECESSION

Latin secessio, means "separated, split off". Here, it refers to the splitting off of particularly young artists from the older generation. Secession was expected to be helpful in the crucial days of historicism. It had its rise by the end of the 19th century and lasted until the end of World War I, protracting into later periods as well. Secession buildings, particularly the representative ones, are complemented with sculptures and paintings, stuccoes, mosaics, gabled creations, marble facings, precious-wood-sorts panelling, metal elements, as well as coloured and etched glass to make up one integral stylistic whole. To the new ornamentalistics belong smoke curves, natural leaves, human masks, circle motives, perpendicular mouldings and carvings. Apart from that, there are non-traditionally shaped gables located over the parts of asymetrically conceived façades. In gables, windows and in diversified façades, complete or uncomplete circle motives occur frequently.

Out of the major Secession monuments are to be mentioned Municipal House of the city of Prague, St. Jan the Nepomuk's church in Štěchovice, railroad station in Prague and others.

MODERNISM

As suggested by the designation itself, this style strived to be a new concept corresponding to tastes and requirements of contemporaneous life. The beginnings of this style in Bohemia date from the period 1905 - 1906 and last until about 1914, when it is stopped by World War I. Its creator in Bohemia was the architect Jan Kotěra. Architectural creation of this period is mainly a space and design, not a shape and adornment-orientated one. Simple geometrical shapes emphasized by intermittance of plaster and brique-stone, along with flat roofs were in vogue. The most important constructions of those days are Kotěra's villa in Prague - Vinohrady dating from the period 1908 - 1909.

CZECH CUBISM AND DECORATIVISM

CUBISM

Originally, Cubism was a trend of French painting art, deriving its name from the Latin term cubus (cube). This was based on the presumption that the cube is the fundamental shape of all bodies. In Czech architecture, Cubism dominates mainly in the second decade of the 20th century. Cubistically conceived buildings were adorned by plastic fronts modelled with crystalline shapes and motives of pyramids and cubes.

Important cubistic monuments are the spa building in Bohdaneč, Black Madonna House in Celetná Street, Prague, villas and houses beneath Vyšehrad and others.

DECORATIVISM - ARCH STYLE

Decorativism accentuates the décor and ornamentalism. Associated with the attribute arch decorativism, it means just the same arch style or style Legiobanka. After World War I former Bank of Czechoslovak legions in Prague, Na Poříčí was erected using this style.

PURISM, CONSTRUCTIVISM AND FUNCTIONALISM

The name **Purism** is derived from Latin purus (pure). In this style purity of architecture deprived of all non-functional, non-organic details, which especially in cubism and decorativism, are considered to be formalistic, are of quite a great impact. Purism, on its part finds these details superfluous.

In modern architecture, **constructivism**, mainly based on the counstruction, makes the latter visible in the final realization of the object.

Functionalism emphasizes the function of the object, its practical utilization in accordance with the purpose the object was intended and erected for.

Both the constructivism and functionalism mostly penetrate or overleap each other, putting themselves through primarily since the twenties and thirties of the 20th century until the outbreak of World War II. New materials, such as armoured, concrete and glass are used. The outer parts of buildings are either plastered or lined with ceramics (e.g. building of the General Pension Institute Prague). In other instances, the outer walls are made of first-quality burnt brickstones or, the constructivistic character of the object is accentuated in that the concrete skeleton of the structure remains visible (e.g. objects of Baťa's Zlín).

ARCHITECTURE AFTER WORLD WAR II

Right after World War II, the architecture in our countries continued marching in the footsteps of functionalism. In this period assuming, later on, the name Period of Post-War Urbanism, the concept of housing estates was gradually developing to solve the problem of post-war living shortages. Rows of green-framed tenement houses with flat roofs, e.g. in Zlín or Hradec Králové, arise all around. Since the necessity of continuous housing estates edification did not cease, the new dwellings had to be erected fast with the shortest projections terms possible. In those days arose the so-called bare types, mostly two-storey, separated from each other, lacking any architectural diversification whatsover, that is to say bare in the proper sense of the word (e.g. in Ostrava - Poruba behind the Arch). In the fifties, a special trend, named traditionalism, set on. This trend was to be understood as an effort to illucidate a certain orientation of socialist realism in architecture. Practically, it meant a new inclination toward historism, though, on quite a different basis than in the second half of the 19th century. Typed versatile tenement houses were coated with elements of historical styles (for instance Rennaissance sgraffitoes were mingled with birchlyte plaster. Housing estates or new towns, such as Poruba, Havířov, made up a rectangular street network with regular house blocks.

1958 was a turn in the post-war architecture. Then, we succeeded in putting through our concept of Czechoslovak Pavillion for the World Exposition in Brussels, Expo '58, linked with a restaurant. Since the end of the fifties, architecture started linking up with earlier traditions of the pre-war functionalism and foreign architectural creation. The housing estates assume a new character when compared with those dating from the preceding period. Their projection was based upon several types, different from each other as to shape and height, but also mutual situation. Some houses were built in tandems, others were diagonally turned lacking any courtyards or garden backgrounds whatsoever. Housing blocks were set in green planes weaved by asphalt pavements and service streets. Thus, the traditional notion of a street was practically gone.

CONTENTS

Buchlov

CZECH HISTORY - CHRONOLOGICAL SURVEY

AUTHORS: Jaroslav Krejčíř, Ing. Stanislav Soják

TRANSLATOR: Dr. Jan Mynařík

EDITORS
OF THE CHRONOLOGICAL PART: PhDr. František Spurný CSc., PhDr. Dan Gawrecki CSc.
Mgr. Yvana Fuxová, PhDr. Zdeněk Jirásek CSc.

ILLUSTRATORS: Pavel Alexander Taťoun, Petr Herzig
Zdeněk Skřivánek, Lenka Suchá

LANGUAGE EDITORS: Caren Rewell, Christopher Guilds

PUBLISCHED BY: © INFOA
Address: INFOA, Nová 141, 789 72 Dubicko, Czech Republic

Printed in the Czech Republic
Moravská tiskárna Olomouc, s. r. o.

ISBN 80 - 85836 - 27 - 0